Picture the Past

Life in the Dust Bowl

Sally Senzell Isaacs

Heinemann Library
Chicago, Illinois

© 2002 Reed Educational & Professional Publishing
Published by Heinemann Library,
an imprint of Reed Educational & Professional Publishing,
Chicago, IL
Customer Service 888-454-2279
Visit our website at www.heinemannlibrary.com

Produced for Heinemann Library by
    Bender Richardson White.
Editor: Lionel Bender
Designer and Media Conversion: Ben White
Picture Researcher: Cathy Stastny
Production Controller: Kim Richardson

06 05 04 03 02
10 9 8 7 6 5 4 3 2 1

Printed in Hong Kong

Library of Congress Cataloging-in-Publication Data.
Isaacs, Sally Senzell, 1950-
    Life during the Dust Bowl / Sally Senzell Isaacs.
        p. cm. -- (Picture the past)
Includes bibliographical references (p.   ) and index.
    ISBN 1-58810-248-3 (hb. bdg.)   ISBN 1-58810-413-3 (pbk. bdg.)
    1. Dust storms--Great Plains--History--20th century--Juvenile literature. 2. Droughts--Great Plains--History--20th century--Juvenile literature. 3. Great Plains--Social life and customs--20th century--Juvenile literature. 4. Farm life--Great Plains--History--20th century--Juvenile literature. 5. Great Plains--Social conditions--20th century--Juvenile literature. 6. Depressions--1929--Great Plains--Juvenile literature. (1. Dust storms--Great Plains. 2. Droughts--Great Plains--History. 3. Depressions--1929.) I. Title.
    F595 .I83 2001
    978--dc21
                                    2001000500

Special thanks to Mike Carpenter at Heinemann Library for editorial and design guidance and direction.

Acknowledgments
The producers and publishers are grateful to the following for permission to reproduce copyright material:
Corbis Images: Arthur Rothstein, pages 6, 7, 8, 11, 14; Bettman Archive, pages 13, 22, 23, 26, 27, 28; Bettman Archive/UPI, page 10: Corbis, pages 12, 19, 21. Library of Congress: pages 1, 3, 9, 15 (from Franklin D. Roosevelt Library), 16, 17, 25. Peter Newark's American Pictures: pages 18, 24, 30.
Cover photograph: Library of Congress/Franklin D. Roosevelt Library.

Illustrations on pages 20–21 and 29 by John James.
Map by Stefan Chabluk.
Cover make-up: Mike Pilley, Radius.

Note to the Reader
Some words are shown in bold, **like this.** You can find out what they mean by looking in the glossary.

ABOUT THIS BOOK

This book tells about the daily life of farm families who suffered in America's Dust Bowl from 1931 to 1938. Experts give many reasons why life became so hard for these farmers. They say that farmers ruined the land by planting too many crops. Also, hard times hit the rest of the country and people could not afford to buy the farmers' vegetables and grains. And then came the very worst years, with no rain and strong wind storms.
We have illustrated the book with photographs taken during the Dust Bowl days. We have also included artists' drawings of how people lived in that time.

The Author
Sally Senzell Isaacs is a professional writer and editor of nonfiction books for children. She graduated from Indiana University, earning a B.S. degree in Education with majors in American History and Sociology. For some years, she was the Editorial Director of Reader's Digest Educational Division. Sally Senzell Isaacs lives in New Jersey with her husband and two children.

CONTENTS

The Dust Bowl

"America's Breadbasket!" That is what people have called the farmland in Texas, Oklahoma, Kansas, and Nebraska. Much of the world's wheat is grown there.

But for several years in the 1930s, the wheat did not grow at all. The corn did not grow. Not even the grass grew. During those years, there was no rain. The farm fields turned to dust. Strong winds lifted the dust and blew it everywhere. These dust storms created an area that was called the Dust Bowl.

Look for these
The illustration of a farm boy and girl show you the subject of each double-page story in the book.

The illustration of a farm house highlights panels with facts and figures about everyday life in the Dust Bowl.

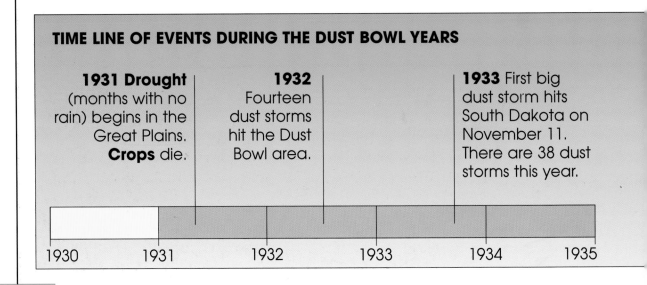

TIME LINE OF EVENTS DURING THE DUST BOWL YEARS

1931 Drought (months with no rain) begins in the Great Plains. **Crops** die.

1932 Fourteen dust storms hit the Dust Bowl area.

1933 First big dust storm hits South Dakota on November 11. There are 38 dust storms this year.

| 1930 | 1931 | 1932 | 1933 | 1934 | 1935 |

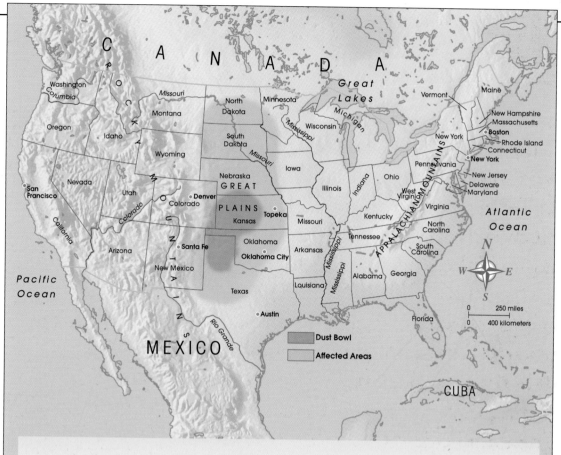

From 1931 to 1938, almost no rain fell in the **Great Plains.** The people in the area known as the Dust Bowl suffered the most. The Dust Bowl included parts of Texas, Oklahoma, Kansas, New Mexico, and Colorado.

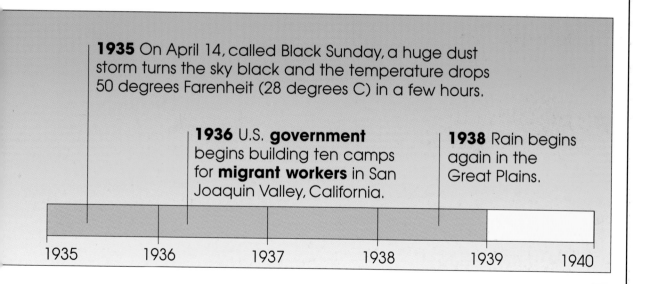

1935 On April 14, called Black Sunday, a huge dust storm turns the sky black and the temperature drops 50 degrees Farenheit (28 degrees C) in a few hours.

1936 U.S. **government** begins building ten camps for **migrant workers** in San Joaquin Valley, California.

1938 Rain begins again in the Great Plains.

1935   1936   1937   1938   1939   1940

On the Farm

The farmers' fields seemed to roll on forever. There were thousands of farms, but they were spread far apart on the **Great Plains**. The closest of neighbors lived miles from each other.

Farmers grew wheat, corn, barley, and oats. They raised animals such as cows, pigs, and chickens.

A farmer and his family lived in a wooden house built on the edge of the fields. The farmer built a barn for his animals. Wheat and corn were stored in other wooden buildings.

This farmer is using a horsedrawn **plow.** The plow breaks up the **soil** and gets it ready for planting seeds.

FASTER PLOWING

Starting in the 1920s, some farmers bought the newest kind of plow. It did not need animals to pull it. It was pulled by a tractor with an engine. Tractors made plowing easier and quicker, but they cost hundreds of dollars.

Many of the farmers grew wheat and sold it to **mills.** Machines at the mill turned the wheat into flour for bread, cakes, and noodles. As long as the weather was good, the farmers grew wheat. As long as people bought bread, the farmers made money.

The Farm House

Most farmers were not rich. Their houses were small with just two or three rooms. Many farmers **borrowed** money from banks to pay for their houses. Some farmers also borrowed money to buy seeds, animals, **plows,** and tractors.

This man and woman are proud of their new farm house. They hope to sell enough wheat, chickens, and eggs to pay for it.

By the 1920s, many farmers had trouble paying the banks for the money they borrowed. Many people in other parts of the United States had lost their jobs and did not have enough money to buy food. Many **mills** stopped buying wheat. Farmers stopped earning money.

Most farm houses had running water but no electric lights or telephones. These children are reading in the main room, which was used as a kitchen, dining room, sitting room, and play room.

No Rain at All

In 1931, more trouble arrived. For months and months, there was no rain. The **crops** stopped growing. The **soil** in the fields dried up into dust. Even the grass turned brown. There was nothing for the farm animals to eat, and they began to die.

As the fields dried up and crops died, the farmers searched the sky for rain clouds, but none came.

HOT AND DRY

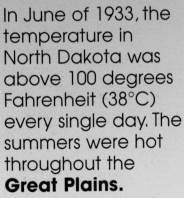

In June of 1933, the temperature in North Dakota was above 100 degrees Fahrenheit (38°C) every single day. The summers were hot throughout the **Great Plains.** People could not waste water on a cool bath or shower.

When there are several months without rain, it is called a **drought**. There had been droughts before the 1930s, and there have been droughts since then. But this one lasted for almost seven years.

This boy's family may need to sell his calf to buy food or to pay for the farm. Children were upset when animals they had grown up with had to be sold.

Black Blizzards

During the worst of the **drought**, the dust storms began. Big gray clouds rolled in. The winds lifted up the dry dirt from the fields and blew it everywhere. The air was black. As people ran home, they could not see their front doors. Sometimes a storm lasted a few hours. Sometimes it lasted a few days.

This Oklahoma farmer sees the dust storm coming. Animals must be rushed into the barn before they get buried by the dust.

Dust blew into eyes and scraped against skin. People ran into their houses. They jammed towels around their doors and windows to try to keep out the dust. But the dust blew in through the tiniest cracks. Parents gave their children wet cloths to put over their faces to keep out the dust. People became sick from breathing in dust.

DUST IN THE DISTANCE

Dust was blown across the United States and out to sea. Sailors in the Atlantic Ocean swept **Great Plains** dust off their ships.

This picture was taken in Kansas City in March 1935. It is the middle of the day, but the sky looks like night. Even with street lights and car lights, it is hard to see through the dust-filled air.

Digging Out

Dust was everywhere. It covered floors and furniture. It settled inside glasses and cups. All the dishes had to be washed. So did shelves and clothes in closets. It took more than a broom to sweep the floors. Sometimes it took a shovel.

Dust filled and piled up against this **shack,** making it unusable.

With no **crops** to sell, farmers sold their tractors and animals. Soon they would have to sell the house and land and leave the **Great Plains.**

After a storm, farmers went outside and dug out buried tools and fences. Sometimes they had to dig out their cars. Many car motors filled with dirt and stopped working. Farmers had no money to repair them. The storms hurt the animals, too. Farm children spent hours cleaning dust from the noses and ears of cows and pigs.

A Child's Life

Children in the Dust Bowl watched their parents worry about money. But they still went to school and took care of the farm animals. Young children fed the pigs, milked the cows, and collected the eggs. Older children helped their parents out in the fields, herding the animals and driving tractors.

HEADING HOME— BACKWARDS

At the first sight of a dust storm, teachers sent students home. On very windy days, children walked backward so the dust would not scratch their faces.

Children learned to play with anything they could find. These two girls are using **tumbleweed** as a bed for their dolls.

Children played games that did not cost money. They hung a rope from a tree and used it as a swing. They played kickball in the yard or jacks on the front porch.

These children are playing on a merry-go-round made from a wooden wagon wheel.

News and Radio

THE WIZARD OF OZ

In 1939, people loved the movie, *The Wizard of Oz*. It tells the story of a poor girl from a farm in Kansas. A **tornado** blows her away to a magical land.

There were no televisions at this time. Farmers got their news and **entertainment** from newspapers, radios, and movies. Everyone who owned a radio had a favorite radio show. Most shows lasted fifteen minutes. They were funny, scary, and exciting.

With a radio, families could listen to news, stories, music, and sports reports. Radios were much larger than they are today.

Most farmers never saw famous baseball teams, such as the New York Yankees. Thanks to radio, they could listen to each pitch and run of a game. Everyone knew about the "home run king," Babe Ruth.

It costs ten cents to see this movie. For the price, these boys will probably see a movie, cartoon, and **newsreel.**

TUESDAYS ADM 10¢

Packing Up

The rain never came. The fields became dryer. The farmers became poorer. Millions of people packed up and left the Dust Bowl. Some sold their houses and land for low prices. Some just walked away from it all. It was time to look for work and schools someplace else. It was time to breathe fresh air.

This family is leaving their farm. They do not know where they will live next. They are homeless.

Children sadly said goodbye to their teachers and friends. Many of their friends had already left. People had heard about the farms in California. Those farmers needed lots of help. It sounded as if everyone could find a job in California. Dust Bowl families headed west.

BIG NUMBERS

During the 1930s, nearly three million people left the Dust Bowl.

Some people did not have cars or trucks. They loaded a few things into wagons or onto carts and wheelbarrows and started walking down the highway.

On the Road

The Dust Bowl families drove for miles and miles. They slept in their cars or on the side of the road. They washed their clothes and their bodies in streams. They went to the bathroom behind bushes. Sometimes they ate only apples for dinner. They saved the cores for another meal.

This old car broke down on the road. The dad might knock on a farmer's door and offer to paint a fence or pick some cherries. That will give him enough money to fix the car and move on.

These workers are picking grapes in California. They will work sixteen hours a day, seven days a week. They will earn four dollars for the week. Children will be paid even less.

NO JOBS

Between 1935 and 1940, more than one million people moved to California. There were too many people and not enough jobs. California had many signs like this one: "If You Are Looking For Work: Keep Out."

There were plenty of farms in California. But soon there were too many workers. Some people found jobs on large farms. They picked grapes, plums, peaches, potatoes, lettuce, or cotton. When the picking was done, the workers had to move.

Farm Camps

Workers who moved from farm to farm were called **migrant workers**. They camped out near the farms where they worked. Some workers lived in tents. Some lived in one-room **shacks** made of cardboard or tin. They slept on the ground and had no bathrooms.

A family of six lived in this homemade shack. Many migrant workers got sick from drinking dirty water and not eating enough food.

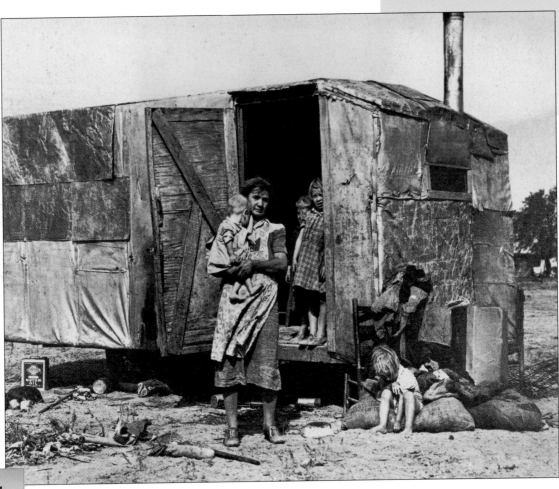

Most cabins at the government camps had no kitchens. Cooks made hot meals. The workers bought breakfast for a penny a day.

In 1936, the United States **government** built camps for the migrant workers. Workers paid a dollar a week for a one-room tent or cabin. The camps had hot showers and toilets. Some had a playground, a baseball diamond, and a school.

School

While the Dust Bowl children traveled to California, they did not go to school. Some of them missed many months or even years. When their parents found work in California, the children started at a new school. But they only stayed there for a few months. When their parents' work was done, they had to move.

This is a **migrant worker** and her two children at a **government** camp at Nipomo, California, in 1936. The family lived in a tent.

These children of migrant workers are at Sunday school in a government camp in Marysville, California. A bus took them to school and church.

SCHOOL LESSONS

- Arithmetic
- Handwriting
- Reading the Bible
- Good manners
- American history
- Sports and games

Many Dust Bowl children had a difficult time at their new schools. They had missed many lessons and could not catch up with the local students. They also were teased for their patched clothing and the way they pronounced their words.

Food

People who had no homes sometimes ate in public parks. Some parks had cooking areas where people could build a fire. Someone put a kettle of water on the fire and others brought food to boil. One person might cook a potato. Another might cook a hot dog.

This family lives in a **government** camp cabin. Instead of chairs, this family sits on boxes when eating at the table.

Migrant Worker Recipe – Meat Stew

Here is a recipe you can make on an outdoor grill or in a campfire. If you do not have an outdoor grill or fire, cook the foil packets in an oven at 350 degrees Fahrenheit (180°C).

WARNING: Do not cook anything unless there is an adult to help you. Always ask an adult to cut the food, build the fire, and place and remove food from the hot coals, grill, or oven.

YOU WILL NEED
For each serving:
2 sheets of aluminum foil each 17 inches (42 centimeters) long and 12 inches (30 centimeters) wide
1 washed and sliced potato
1/2 washed and sliced green pepper
1 washed and sliced carrot
1/4 cup (60 ml) chopped onion
1/4 pound (110 g) ground beef or turkey
1 teaspoon butter
salt and pepper

FOLLOW THE STEPS

1. Have an adult start the fire in the grill or campfire. Let the coals burn down until they are glowing red.
2. Place the two pieces of foil on top of each other. Spread some butter on the top sheet of foil.
3. Place one serving of ground meat on top of the butter in the center of the foil. Flatten it to about 1/2 inch (12 mm) thick.
4. Place the sliced potato, pepper, carrot, and onion on the meat.
5. Sprinkle salt, pepper, and the rest of the butter on the vegetables.
6. Wrap the doubled piece of foil over the food. Fold the ends a few times to keep the juices from spilling out.
7. Put the foil packet, folded sides up, on the grill, on the coals, or in the oven. Cook 1 hour.

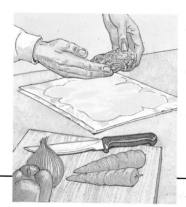

Rain in the Dust Bowl

At last, after seven long years, the clouds opened up over the Dust Bowl. Finally, there were enough rainy days to make the **crops** grow. Farmers who had stayed planted seeds in their fields again. Some farmers came back from California and other places. Others decided to stay away. They had found new jobs, new friends, and new homes.

After the Dust Bowl years, farmers started planting their fields in ways that would keep the rain water in the **soil** and keep the soil from blowing away. Today, the **Great Plains** once again produce huge amounts of grain. Here, grain is being harvested from fields.

Glossary

borrow to use something that belongs to someone else, with permission

crop plant grown for food

drought several months, or longer, without rain

entertainment things to do for fun, such as listening to the radio or watching a movie or a ballgame

government people who make laws and decisions for the people

Great Plains land between the Mississippi River and Rocky Mountains. It is mostly flat or gently rolling land.

migrant worker person who moves around to work jobs as they are needed

mill building where things, such as flour or clothing, are made using the power of wheels driven by wind or flowing water

newsreel short film about what is happening in the world. It was shown at movie theaters before the days of television.

plow farm machine used to turn over the soil before seeds are planted

shack small hut or house made quickly and cheaply

soil dirt or earth in which plants grow

tornado very strong whirling wind and funnel-shaped cloud that moves over the land

tumbleweed bushy plant that dries up and blows around in the wind

More Books to Read

Wroble, Lisa A. *Kids During the Great Depression.* New York: Rosen Publishing Group, 1999.

An older reader can help you read this book:

Stanley, Jerry. *Children of the Dust Bowl: The True Story of the School at Weedpatch Camp.* New York: Crown Books for Young Readers, 1992.

Index

Macramé Accessories

PATTERNS AND IDEAS FOR KNOTTING

Dona Z. Meilach

CROWN PUBLISHERS, INC.
NEW YORK

Other Books by Dona Z. Meilach
in Crown's Arts and Crafts Series

Macramé; Creative Design in Knotting
Papier-Mâché Artistry
Contemporary Stone Sculpture
Contemporary Art with Wood
Direct Metal Sculpture
  with Donald Seiden

Also:

Contemporary Leather: Art Accessories
Creating Art from Anything
Creating with Plaster
Making Contemporary Rugs and Wall Hangings
Printmaking
Papercraft
Accent on Crafts
Creative Stitchery
  with Lee Erlin Snow
Collage and Found Art
  with Elvie Ten Hoor

© 1972 by Dona Z. Meilach
Library of Congress Catalog Card Number:
78–185074

Printed in the United States of America
Published simultaneously in Canada by
General Publishing Company Limited

Designed by Margery Kronengold

Second Printing, April, 1972

Contents

Foreword and Acknowledgments

Macramé, the revival of an ancient method of knotting cords, has captured the interest of everyone who likes to create beautiful things from fibers. It is versatile, adaptable, and simple to do with striking results. *Macramé Accessories* is designed for the person who wants to follow patterns and for craftsmen seeking ideas for original items and designs in this fascinating knotting medium.

Actual cords used, amounts needed, and step-by-step directions are provided for several pieces in this book. However, experience has shown that with many objects the knotting "grows as you work" and objects are more easily used as inspiration for individual knotting projects. Many of the examples are offered to inspire you to work in various ways and adapt the ideas to your own pieces.

The approach is to be creative; to feel free to digress from any given pattern and make it individually yours. You will gain the satisfaction of having created something original.

Basic knotting instructions are presented in Chapter 2; use of other knot variations and methods for increasing are shown throughout the book; use Chapter 9 as a reference for additional knotting hints.

My sincere thanks to all knotters who have contributed to this book. As my deadline approached, it was a delight to receive shipments of magnificent Macramé to be photographed and returned to artists all over the country. Each knotter's name accompanies the work. Only lack of space prevents me from using more of the over five hundred pieces that were sent.

My gratitude to Susan and Al Meilach who helped in many ways. Special thanks to my husband, Mel, who assisted me with photography in our studio and in settings anywhere my whimsy dictated.

Dona Z. Meilach

NOTE: *All photos by Dona and Mel Meilach unless otherwise credited.*

Macramé Accessories

PATTERNS AND IDEAS FOR KNOTTING

Macramé accessories are attractive, different, fun to make, and exciting to wear. Skirt for the Shy Hot Pants Wearer designed by Eileen Bernard. Peace Symbol necklace by Shirley Volpe.

Macramé
Materials and
Methods

Among the many attractive aspects of Macramé is that the materials are minimal, easy to find, inexpensive, and portable. The two readily learned knots, the Clove Hitch and Square Knot, can be tied in infinite pattern arrangements to make a stunning variety of objects.

Add to all this the fact that the knots and their appearance, once learned, are so easy to recognize that a pattern can be "read" from a picture more quickly than from lengthy word directions. Therefore, the best approach to Macramé is to learn the Clove Hitch and Square Knot. Then make one or two sample projects using the specific directions given. After that, it's an easy step to emulate any item shown and to develop your own ideas for cord, color, and design combinations.

Materials needed are cord, pins, scissors, and a knotting surface. Cords such as jute, cotton, manila, sisal, wool, and synthetics are available at hardware and dime stores, Macramé and weaving suppliers, marine and cordage companies, millinery suppliers, department store drapery and yarn counters, or anywhere you find them. Suitable Macramé cords are the same as those used for household and industrial purposes including nylon and cotton seine twine, chalk line, navy cord, wrapping twine, gift wrap cord, knotting and rug yarns, Swistraw, yacht braid, upholsterer's cord—the list is endless.

A knotting surface is any material that will accept T and U pins to hold the work in place. Use a polyfoam pad about 12 inches square, thick cardboard held to a clipboard, a square of Celotex or soft pine wood, or any surface you can improvise such as a couch cushion, mattress, or throw pillow. Once familiar with knot tying, you can work from a spring curtain rod in a doorway, by holding the beginning knot around your toe, from ends stuffed into a drawer, mounted over a dressmaker's dummy, and other ways you'll devise for efficiently knotting a specific project.

It's wise to knot a three- to six-inch square of a cord before embarking on an ambitious project. First, many color cords are available but not all are colorfast. A blue purse that gets caught in the rain can ruin a dress if the color runs. Wash cord to test for color fastness. You can dye cords with any yarn and fabric dye but these, too, should be washed to be sure colors are fast.

Second, test cords for shrinkage. Draw an outline of the knotted sample on paper, wash and dry the piece, then remeasure against the drawing. If the washed knotting is appreciably smaller, adjust size for shrinkage or plan to have garment dry cleaned.

Third, where size is critical, use the sample as a knotting gauge just as one makes a sample knitting gauge. Determine how many cords make an inch on the horizontal holding line, then multiply the number of inches by the number of cords. For example: if six Lark's Head mounts equal one inch, that means three cords equal one inch (each Lark's Head is one cord doubled). For an eight-inch width you would require 3×8, or 24 cords (48 knotting strands).

Materials for Macramé include any cord you like for knotting a particular item; T and U pins to hold work to knotting board of polyfoam, cork, Celotex, carpet square or soft pine; scissors, tape measure, beads, and wire for stringing beads. A plastic circle template is convenient for measuring cord diameters. Dowels and curtain rods hold mounted cords. Also handy are matches, needles, and thread.

Determining necessary lengths of cords is always iffy. A general rule is to think of each length required as four times the finished knotting length. This means that each cord from the mounting to the end is four times the length of the finished piece; however, when measuring cords that are *doubled* on the holding line, measure *eight times the finished length*. It might help if you think of:

Knotting *cords* as the full length of cord needed before doubling or eight times the finished length.

Knotting *strands* as the length of each piece from the holding line to the end or four times finished length.

Naturally, loosely knotted projects require shorter pieces. Thicker diameter cords require more length. With experience you'll be able to estimate cord needs readily.

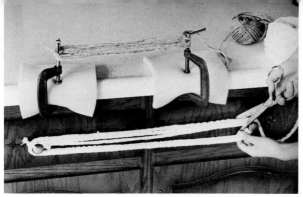

1

2

3

1. An easy way to measure is by winding cord lengths around drawer handles or between two C-clamps mounted on a table or counter, then cut at one side. Protect counter tops with a piece of foam. Always allow more cord rather than less.

2. For three-dimensional objects, knot cords over a wig stand or around a plastic container that you can poke pins into. Clothes may be worked over a dressmaker's dummy, pillow tied to body shape, or a mannequin. Some items can be knotted flat with the pattern drawn on the knotting board, then the sides knotted together as seams. A spring tension curtain rod, rear, holds knotting straight, is adjustable, and may be moved from one doorway or knotting spot to another.

3. Knotting boards may be marked off in one-inch squares to facilitate even knotting patterns.

4. Three-dimensional knotting for purses, ponchos, and similar shapes may be done over a chair back with cardboard inserted if pinning is necessary. Several layers of cardboard or a polyfoam pillow may also be strung for a tubular piece and no seams are required.

5. A handle or a dowel tied to a nail on a wall may also be improvised. Use any working setup so long as it makes the knotting progress in an efficient manner.

4

5

Basic Knots and Procedures

The two basic Macramé knots are the Clove Hitch and Square Knot. Cords are mounted on a horizontal holding line such as another length of cord, or a rod, with a Lark's Head Knot, and the work is held taut while knotting. For some projects, other beginning methods illustrated may be used.

When Knotting, We Will Refer to "Knotting Cords" and "Knotting Strands" as Those Which Are Tied in Knots. "Anchor Cords" Are Those Around Which Knots Are Tied.

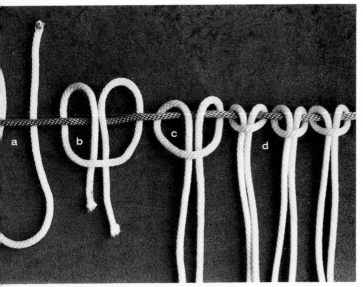

1. The Lark's Head is used for mounting cords across a holding line such as a length of cord, dowel, curtain rod, twig, or braided cords.
   a. Fold cord in half and place loop under horizontal holding line from the top down.
   b. Reach under loop and over the horizontal line and grasp the two loose ends; bring them down through the loop.
   c. Pull and tighten.
   d. Finished knots.

2. The Overhand Knot is an efficient way to begin long sennits (lengths of knotted cords) for belts, jewelry, and straps. Grasp all cords together, make a loop, and pull end cords through the loop. When you want a long group of unknotted cords at the beginning of a belt, make the Overhand Knot the desired length from the end of the cord. To work, pin the knot to a board, tie over a doorknob, around a chair leg, place under a brick, or your foot, and begin to knot in a pattern.

a. The shape of the holding line determines the shape of a project. A pointed holding line is used to begin the tab end of a belt. For necklines and armholes the holding line, pinned to the pattern outline, becomes the edge of the garment.

b. You can work from the end of a piece using single strands of cords. Simply pin each cord to your knotting surface as shown and begin to Clove Hitch or Square Knot along cord. This eliminates the Lark's Head Mounting and permits a fringe at each end of the work.

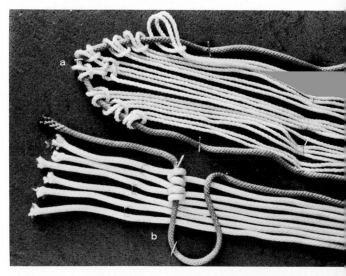

Working from the center to each side of a project makes it easy to match patterns and determine lengths. It also means working with shorter lengths of cord. This method is particularly good for belts and neckpieces. Find the center of the cords and pin them to the board; then use the knots desired and work in both directions from the center out.

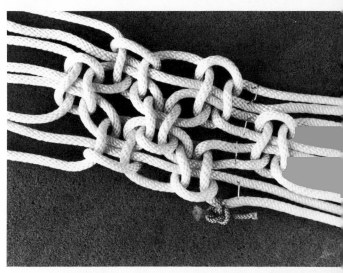

To begin a round project for hats, doilies, hangings, tablecloths, and similar items, pin a rubber or plastic ring or a cord shaped into a circle to the holding board. Attach the knotting cords with a Lark's Head and proceed with the knotting pattern. When Clove Hitching over a center circular cord, extend the end of this center cord as the anchor cord for subsequent Clove Hitch rows.

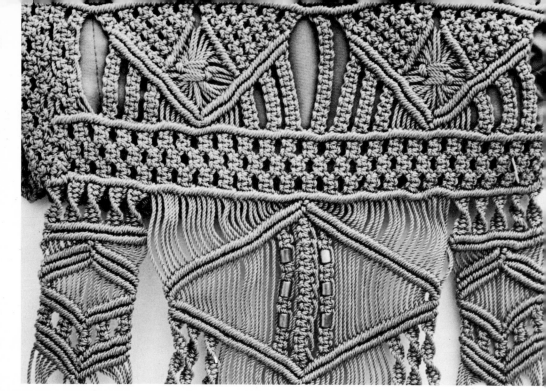

Entire pattern tied with variations of the two basic Macramé knots: the Clove Hitch results in the horizontal and diagonal bars; the Square Knot is the fill pattern in different numerical combinations. Once you learn to tie the knots, you'll be able to identify them and you can read a pattern without requiring line-by-line directions.

Belt of polypropylene Macra-Cord is designed completely with repeat patterns of Horizontal and Diagonal Clove Hitches. Seven 10-foot-long cords are used for knotting. An eighth cord, 14 feet long, is used for the anchor because the anchor cord shortens more rapidly than the knotting strands. (Winkie T. Fordney)

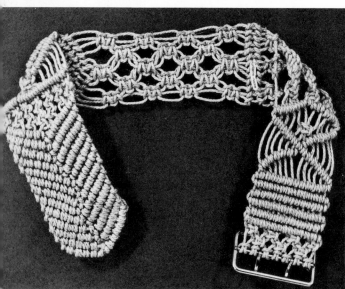

Belt of manila cord is tied with Diagonal and Horizontal Clove Hitches for bars. A pattern of Alternating Square Knots creates the open lacy pattern. The seven-cord mounting (14 strands) is switched to Square Knots using 4 cords at each side and 6 cords for the center knot pattern. Square Knot patterns are usually worked in multiples of four cords but any number of cords can be adjusted in a design. (Berni Gorski)

CLOVE HITCH

The Clove Hitch is made by tying two loops over an anchor cord. The direction of the anchor cord determines the angle of the Clove Hitch bar—horizontal or diagonal. It may also be tied vertically or in a curve.

HORIZONTAL CLOVE HITCH →
Left to right:

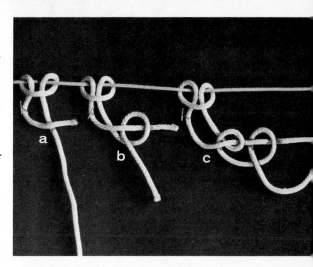

a. Pin left strand of the first cord as shown and place it on top of all the cords. This becomes the "anchor cord" around which each strand will be knotted in turn. Always begin the knotting strand <u>under</u> the anchor cord and hold or pin the anchor cord taut.

b. Bring the knotting strand from under the anchor, loop it over and around to the left and through the loop as shown. This is the first half of the Clove Hitch. Tighten the loop.

c. The second half of the knot is made to the right of the first loop. It begins over the anchor cord, loops around to the left and through as shown.

Continue to tie each strand individually around the anchor cord using the two loops of the Clove Hitch. As each loop is tied, push it next to the previous loop. An Overhand Knot tied in the end of the anchor cord will help you identify it. Always keep the anchor cord taut so knots are tied **over** it and not with it.

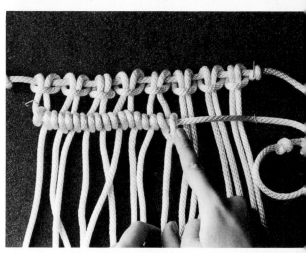

HORIZONTAL CLOVE HITCH →
Right to left:

To create a second bar the Clove Hitch is tied in reverse using the same anchor cord pinned or held taut across all the strands.

a. Place the anchor cord over the knotting strands. Begin knotting with the first strand on right, next to the anchor cord.

b. Loop knotting strand from under the anchor, around, over and through as shown. Tighten.

c. Begin knotting strand over anchor cord and to left of the first half of the knot for the second loop, working it around and through as shown. Tighten. Continue to tie each strand individually around the anchor.

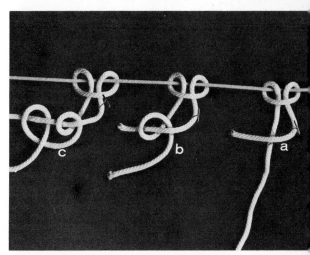

The completed two horizontal bars will appear like this.

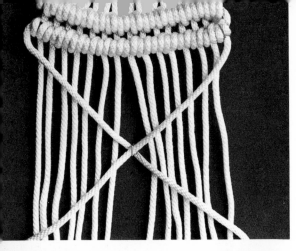

DIAGONAL CLOVE HITCH

To make diagonal bars, the same Clove Hitches are used, but the angle at which the anchor cord is held changes. The direction of the anchor cord determines the direction of the Hitches. Anchor cords may be changed at any point to alter the direction of the row, to make a wavy design or whatever is desired. Bars may be made in as many multiples as you like, either close together or far apart.

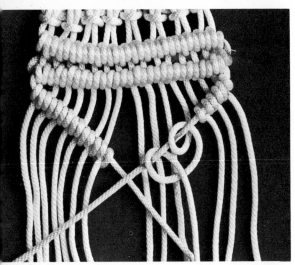

Pin the cord to the board in the diagonals desired: here the diagonal form is an X shape. Clove Hitch from each side, being careful to keep your knotting strands in the proper order.

Beginning with the outer strands, Clove Hitches are tied from left to right on the left diagonal anchor cord; and from right to left on the opposite side. Any cord may become a new anchor cord any place or direction in the knotting.

Continue the direction of each leg to make an X shape. Cross the anchor cords at the center and continue to Clove Hitch each cord from the center out.

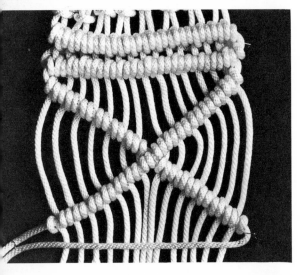

Finished X pattern with the anchor cord pinned to accept the next horizontal bar. The bars act as organizing elements for design.

For a diamond pattern, pick up the two center cords and pin one to each edge. Clove Hitch each strand from the center out, then pin the cords to form a V shape. Clove Hitch over these from each side and a diamond design results.

VERTICAL CLOVE HITCH   →

Left to right:
The Clove Hitch also may be tied vertically. For Vertical Hitches, the cord formerly used for the anchor changes its role and becomes the knotting cord. Because this one cord is used continuously for knotting it is used up very rapidly. When planning pieces with Vertical Clove Hitches, make the knotting cord much longer than any other cord. Each vertical cord, in turn, serves as an anchor cord for the vertical Clove Hitch. Vertical Hitching usually follows horizontal bars.

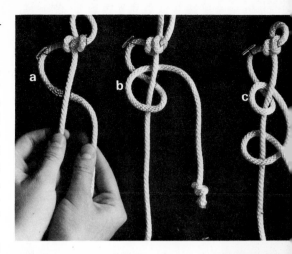

a. Place a pin at left edge of the work to hold the knotting cord. Bring the knotting cord (formerly the anchor cord) under the first vertical strand on the left.

b. Loop the knotting cord over the new vertical anchor to the front, then around and through for the first half of the knot.

c. The second half of the knot is looped over the vertical cord and around as shown.

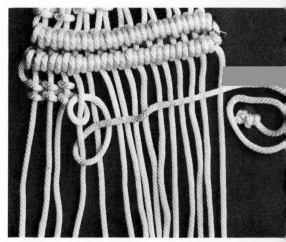

Continue the Vertical Clove Hitch by placing the knotting cord under each vertical strand and Clove Hitching with the same cord each knot.

VERTICAL CLOVE HITCH   →

Right to left:
This involves exactly the opposite procedure from that described above.

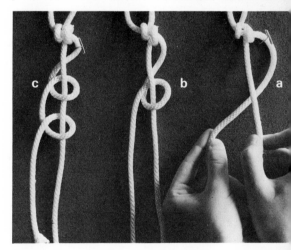

a. Pin the knotting cord at the right edge of the work and bring the knotting cord under the vertical strand at the right.

b. Loop the knotting cord to the right over the vertical strand, around and through at the top of the loop.

c. Make the second half of the Hitch over the anchor to the right, around the top of the loop and through. Continue by bringing the knotting cord under each strand and repeating the directions of the loops for the knot until the row is completed.

Finished rows of Vertical Clove Hitches appear like this. They may be tightened. When one cord is used for knotting it shortens very rapidly. If necessary, introduce a new cord to begin the next row by pinning it to the board. Later you can tie, stitch, or glue these ends together at the back of the work.

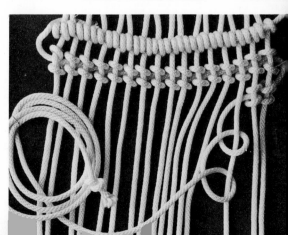

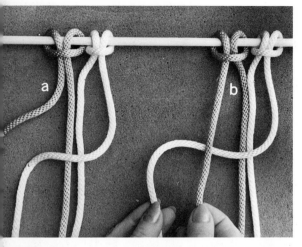

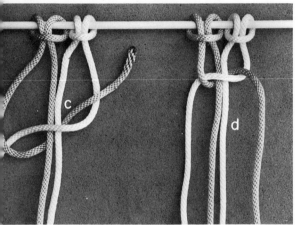

THE SQUARE KNOT

The Square Knot, the second basic Macramé knot, is usually tied with four cords. The two inside cords serve as anchor cords for the two outside knotting cords. Square Knot patterns appear infinite; they may be tied loosely or tightly; in any multiples, long and short. Mounting cords in amounts divisible by four such as 12, 16, 20, 24, 32, 48, simplifies Square Knotting patterns. You may also vary the number of anchor and knotting cords.

To tie the Square Knot, follow the steps shown. They involve the same procedure, first to the left of the anchors, and then to the right. Or you can tie the right side first and then the left to balance the appearance of the knot ridge on a symmetrical piece.

a. Begin with four cords. Bring the right cord over and to the left of the two anchor cords.
b. Place the left cord over the right cord.
c. Bring the left cord under the anchors and up through the loop formed by the right cord.
d. Pull, and you have the first half of the Square Knot.

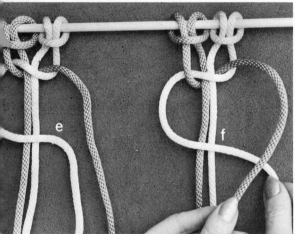

e. For the second half of the knot: bring the left cord over and to the right of the two anchor cords and place the right cord over it.
f. Bring the right cord under the anchors and up through the loop formed by the left cord.

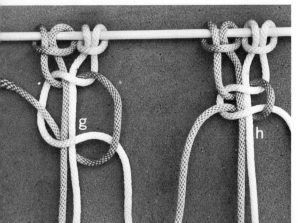

g. Pull the cords and . . .
h. The finished knot.

THE HALF KNOT TWIST

1. The attractive twisted sennits used to such advantage in accessory design are made by repeating one half only of the Square Knot either to the left or right of the anchors; hence it is called the Half Knot. The sennit begins to twist after about the fourth Half Knot. Continue to work the Half Knot, always tying to the same side of the anchors until the desired number of twists result.

2. Examples of Half Knot Twist sennits.

3. Tying Square Knot sennits is simplified if anchor cords are held taut. You can wrap them around a pin at the bottom of your board when thin cords are used; for working heavier cords many people like to keep a hook at their waist for quickly anchoring the cords. These hooks are specially designed for Macramé; the wood hook is simple to make; put a hole in one end; a hook at the other; put a cord through the hole and tie it at your waist. The metal hook slips over a belt. A skeleton key tied around the waist will also do the trick. Be sure the work is held taut. A hook may also be clamped at the front of the work.

4. Beads are a popular decorative adjunct. They are simply slid up cords and held in place by knots. Beads must have large enough holes to string on cords. A piece of very thin wire used as a needle threader facilitates work with small beads and thin cord. A leather lacing needle may be used to string thicker cords as only one strand is clamped to the needle end to be fed through the beads. Beads may be placed anywhere in the knotting on either Square Knot or Clove Hitch cords.

1

2

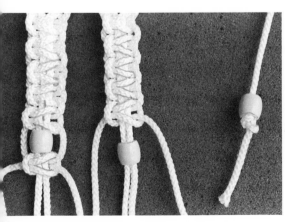

4

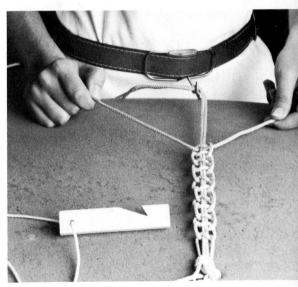

3

THE ALTERNATING SQUARE KNOT

Probably the most useful Square Knot variation is the Alternating Square Knot. It is simple to do, easy to vary, and so attractive that it is basic to all Macramé accessories. Study the pattern at the right as you read the directions. Or, to make a lacy dress decoration as shown below, place cords directly on the page, pinning the holding line off the sides and top of the book onto your knotting board. You will have to pin out the curves of the scallops on the sides.

Use a stiff cord so it will hold the shape of the curves. Cut a doubled cord for a holding line long enough to go around your neck. Measure six cords (12 strands yield $12 \div 4 = 3$ sets of Square Knots); each should be approximately twice your height if you want a floor-length accessory, shorter for a hem length. Double the cords and mount on holding line with Lark's Heads.

Follow the pattern and tie the first row of Square Knots loosely, beginning with the first four cords. For the second row, *drop* the first two cords, *then Square Knot with the next four cords*. Knot each next group of four cords until the row is completed with two cords remaining at the end.

For the third row, pick up the first four cords again at the left and knot as in the first row, being careful to pin the curves to the board to hold them as in the pattern. Continue the pattern for nine rows, add a dab of white glue at the back bottom of each knot to hold it tight; then add crow beads at varying distances over one or two cords holding the beads in place with an Overhand Knot. The piece may be tacked to a dress or tied around the neck as jewelry.

The Alternating Square Knot tied loosely results in a lacy, scalloped edge pattern. Lily Macra-Cord, a polypropylene, retains the shapes of the knots when they are loosely tied. Variations result by tying two or three knots before alternating or by knotting closer together rather than so far apart. (Dona Meilach)

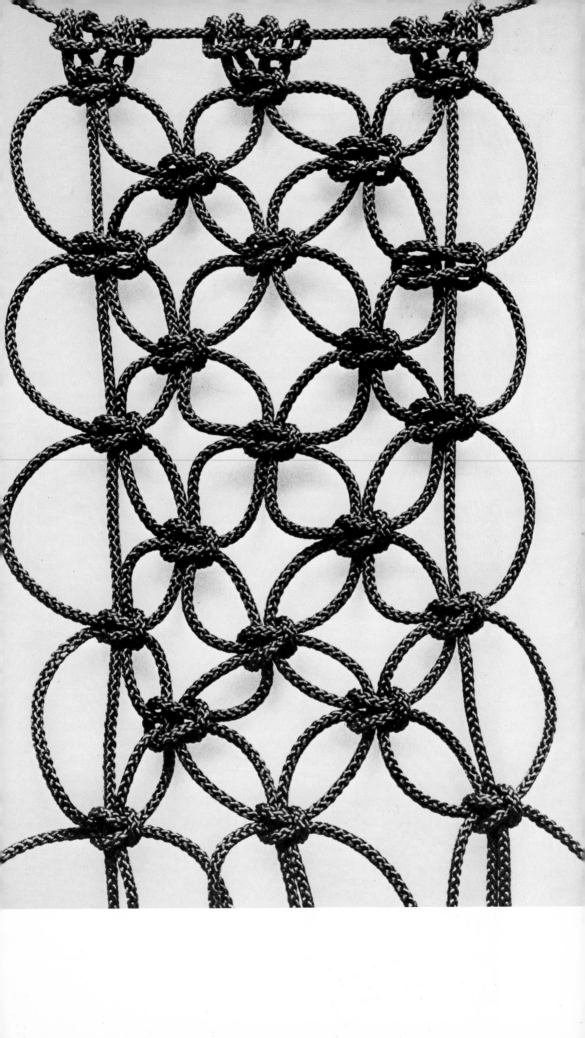

Belts and Other Smart Trappings

Belts are practical and easy initial knotting projects. A belt width is determined by the diameter of the cord and the number of cords mounted for tying. A belt may be simply a sennit of Half Knot Twists, all Square Knots made with four or more cords, or all Diagonal Clove Hitches. Once you've made a sennit belt, you are ready to develop more interesting designs using one or both basic knots. Follow the patterns of illustrated belts but feel free to add your own interpretations, combinations of colors, textures, cords, beads, and buckles.

If belts are knotted from a grouped Overhand Knot (page 10) at one end, or from the center out, figure cord lengths at four times the size of the waist plus fringe. If doubled cords are mounted on a buckle bar or begun from the tab end (page 11), then cut cords eight times the waist size. With thicker cords, figure two additional lengths. If minimal knotting is combined with floating (unknotted) areas, then you will need less cord. When in doubt, knot a sample using about a 36-inch knotting length doubled and figure how long a sennit this will yield, then multiply.

Beads, shells, bones, and other unusual findings make interesting details for belts. Use plastic bracelets, plastic cabone rings, buckles from old belts, shoes, and purses, and any other adaptable items. The more imaginative findings you add to Macramé accessories, the more unusual they will be. Think in terms of designing a new belt to change the appearance of a dress or pants. A belt without buckles may be converted into a long neckpiece by tying the two parts together with an Overhand or Josephine Knot. You may slide a ring or scarf holder over the two ends to hold them together for a necktie also.

The same belt patterns may be combined in suspenders for men and women, as shown. Belts make wonderful gifts for everyone, young and old.

Belt of seine twine is combined with rings and beads painted to match. Note that the cords are mounted from the rings in two directions and knotting continues. To eliminate loose fringe from the back ring, one set of ends is worked back under the knots with a crochet hook. (Jeanette Cohen)

Suspenders are made by knotting two belt lengths together at the back for a crossover. Suspenders are clipped at the back with suspender snaps available at sewing counters. Loose front ends are tied to a belt or belt loops and allowed to hang. Marietta wears bright yellow suspenders made of rattail cord completely Diagonal Clove Hitched. Each side uses six lengths of four yards for knotting and one five-yard length for the anchor cord. Knotting may begin at one end, or from the center shoulder and worked in both directions. Before completing the lengths, combine them at the rear as shown in pair B. Pair A is made of Square Knots with beads. (Neva Humphreys)

BELT FOR SHY HOT PANTS WEARER

To make the revealing but subtle swishy Belt for Shy Hot Pants Wearer, you will need:

Ten 22-foot lengths of No. 18 nylon twist cord

Eighteen six-foot lengths of 1/4-inch-diameter nylon twist cord (about 1/16 inch diameter)

Several dozen white crow beads.

Begin with the ten thinner cords from a grouped Overhand Knot pinned to your knotting surface. (Later you untie the Overhand Knot and wrap the ends to match.) Follow the pattern of Diagonal Clove Hitch and Alternating Square Knots, putting beads on as you work. Knot for about three inches. (Detail A)

Next, fold thick cord in half, pin to your board so that the loop extends above belt cords; Clove Hitch three sets of loops into the work (Detail B). Thick cords should extend to about knee length.

String rows of eight beads on top, bottom, and center double strands as shown below. Measure the pattern of tied-in thick strands and beads to determine how many patterns you will need for your waist size, allowing for the tie in front. Then repeat four to six patterns as necessary. Finish the second end to match the first. Untie the grouped Overhand Knot and wrap each end (see pages 87–88 for wrapping) and leave fringe for tie. Unravel twist of heavy cord all around. (Eileen Bernard)

Detail A   Detail B

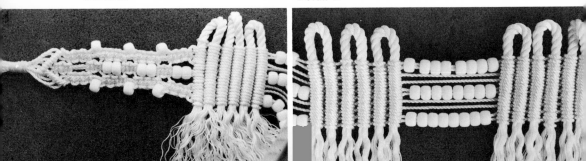

HALTER OF GREEN AND WHITE NYLON CORD

Belt—*Make the belt first, beginning at the back using eight four-yard lengths of green nylon cord attached to a six-inch cord holding line. Work the design using Clove Hitches but make the center front panel in all Alternating Square Knots as shown.*

Bib—*Double sixteen two-yard lengths of white cord and attach with a Lark's Head to the belt front top edge in the spaces between Square Knots. Use four green cords at each end and eight white cords in the center.*

Work nine rows of Alternating Square Knots, two rows of Clove Hitches, then three more rows of Alternating Square Knots. In the next row, make a Square Knot Button (page 90) in each green section and in the white section as shown (for tassle), then three more rows of Alternating Square Knots and three rows of Clove Hitches to finish the top of the bib. Loose ends are folded behind the work, cut to about 1 1/2 inches, pulled back through underside of the knots with a crochet hook, and bound off with bias tape or stitched to the back.

Straps—*Cut twelve five-yard lengths of green. Double and attach six lengths to each side of the bib at the outer edge of the green panel with the Lark's Head over the Clove Hitched line. Work the straps in a pattern to match the belt. Make the straps long enough to cross over in back and attach to the belt with large hooks and eyes sewn in or with short pieces of Velcro Zipper tape. Finish the inside edges of the belt and straps by tucking the loose ends under and stitching on bias tape.*

Make the front chain detail six inches long using four 18-inch lengths of green cord with tassles at the end. Lace through Square Knot Buttons.
(Eileen Bernard)

WAIST CINCHER BELTS

Penelope Laing shares her methods for creating one-of-a-kind belts. She says, "No matter how much detailed instructions one reads, it is almost impossible for two people to make two belts exactly alike; even I can't make two identical." Follow the general instructions and ideas on the next pages, then create belts that are really your own originals. Design as many style variations as you like.

Use a 3/32- to 1/8-inch cord such as parachute braid (from Army/Navy stores), cotton or nylon braid, or Lily Macra-Cord made of polypropylene. The advantage of polypropylene and some other synthetic cords is that short ends can be "welded" by heating them with a match or a hot metal tool and pushing the ends together until the heat fuses them. Depending upon knotting you will need 100 to 150 yards of cord. Penny does her knotting on a soft board of Celotex or Hemosote.

Belts are made in two halves, then knotted together at the back and laced in front.

For each half cut a holding line about eight inches long and pin to the board. Use a Lark's Head to mount eight lengths of knotting cord, each about five times the length of the waist measurement. Clove Hitch the first row for support as later the Lark's Head will be undone for lacing. However, too many rows of Clove Hitches tend to make the belts too stiff, but a few rows every few inches prevent curling.

Continue to knot following any patterns illustrated, increasing the cords for width where necessary by working additional lengths into the Clove Hitch bars (page 13) and in the Square Knots (page 16). Knot each belt half about 1 1/2 inches shorter than half the waist measurement because cords stretch and they look better when laced tightly.

Make two matching belt halves, then pin backs (Lark's Head mountings will be fronts) close together on your board and knot the cords from each half together at back with a hard knot that will fit the design, either Clove Hitching or Square Knotting from opposite sides. Clip the loose ends to about two inches and work into the underside of knots with a crochet hook, adding a touch of white glue or stitching if they jump out.

Finish the front by pulling out the holding cord and undoing the Lark's Heads so they form loops. Cut one or more lengths of cord about one yard and lace through the opened Lark's Head loops. Tie.

Similar belts may be designed in one piece; they may be tied in the back or may incorporate different types of ties and hardware. Large brass eyelets may be put on the Lark's Head before knotting and used for lacing too. (Photos, Richard Laing)

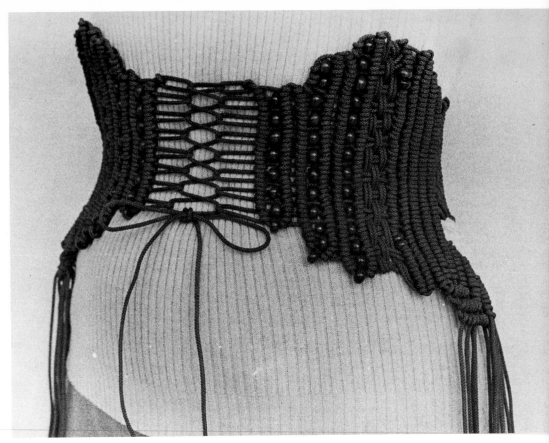

Cinch belt made of Lily Macra-Cord incorporates easy-to-follow weaving with Horizontal and Diagonal Clove Hitches and beads. Extended side panels result from new long cords added as anchors, knotting them and letting the ends hang at the sides after the knotting function is finished. (Penelope Laing; Photo, Richard Laing)

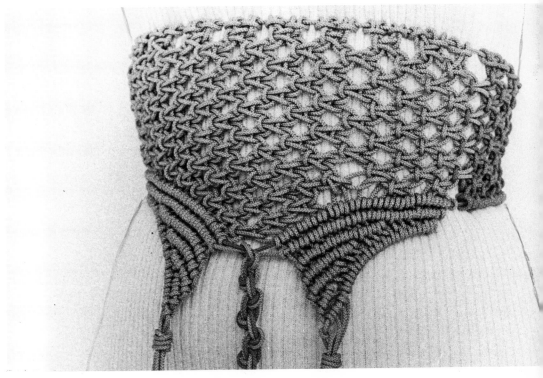

This belt is made from the top down: a holding line several inches longer than the waist measurement is used for mounting cords that are worked downward and all around. New anchor cords added at the bottom are brought around to the back and the belt is tied at the back. (Penelope Laing; Photo, Richard Laing)

In the three belts pictured on these two pages, Penelope Laing incorporates the Alternating Half Hitch Chain illustrated below. (Belt photos, Richard Laing)

ALTERNATING HALF HITCH CHAIN

The Half Hitch is one loop (or the first half) of the Clove Hitch. Tie one loop only of the left strand over the right strand, then alternate and tie one loop of the right over the left. This alternating Half Hitch chain may be used with one, two, or more strands and tied close together or far apart.

Alternating Half Hitches, Horizontal Clove Hitches, and beads are used. (Penelope Laing; Photo, Richard Laing)

The same as above without the beads but with an Overhand Knot detail in the center back.

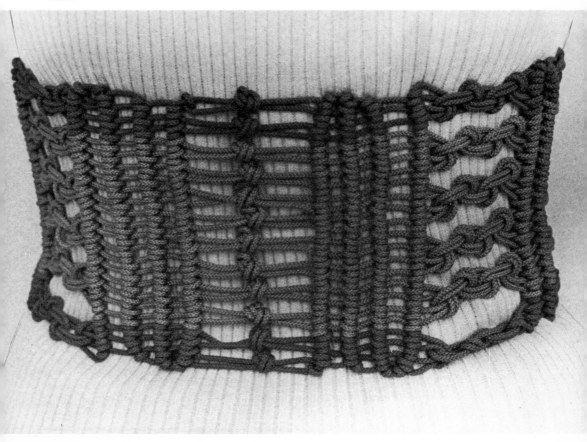

MORE BELT IDEAS

1. A sennit of Square Knots combines two lengths of knitting worsted and two lengths of No. 30 seine twine. Loops are formed by pinning out the knotting cords before tying each knot. Shapes of leather and fur are tied in. (Virginia Black; Photo, artist)

2. Unusual detailing of Alternating Square Knots, Horizontal Clove Hitches, and floating cords may be used for belts for men and women. For front view, see below.

3. Front of the white cable cord belt above: repeats the diamond shape and has a braided cascading tie ending with Wrapping and Overhand Knots. (Henry Majinn; Photo, Hildyne Manpearl)

4. Wide hip-hugger belt of white No. 24 seine twine begins from the eight doubled cords over the holding line (right), and is tied with Alternating Square Knots. The left end is finished with Square Knots and the loose cords are unraveled. To wear, simply tie the holding cords with the Square Knot cords. (Sandra Harrison)

5. The same knotting ideas used for belts can be shortened and worked from a ring for a key chain. Key chains may also be added to belts. (Jeanette Cohen)

6. Leather strips knotted loosely in the Alternating Square Knot pattern have a beautiful texture, are springy, and will stretch to any size, yet never lose their shape. (Creative Leathers by Roberta)

7. Unusual findings (hardware) may be devised from found objects. For this belt, the buckle is a length of bone with a hole drilled at the top. The bone is slipped through loops purposely designed in the other end of the belt. (Winkie T. Fordney; Photo, Virginia Black)

8. Yarn belt is worked from plastic bracelet rings. Extra cord mountings are added for the front hangings and ties. (Jeanette Cohen)

9. Cummerbund of white and red dyed cotton seine twine illustrates variations possible with only Clove Hitches and Square Knots. (Lois Constantine; Photo, Virginia Black)

10. Beads worked into extended loops of Square Knotted cords add interest and texture to a belt. (Winkie T. Fordney; Photo, Virginia Black)

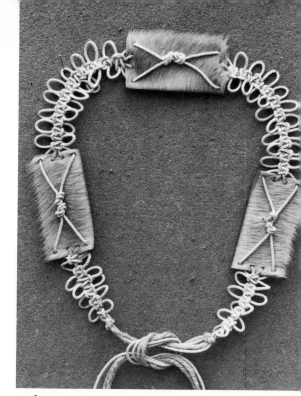

1

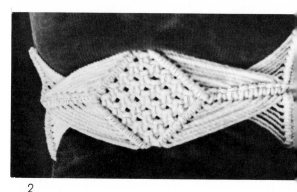

2

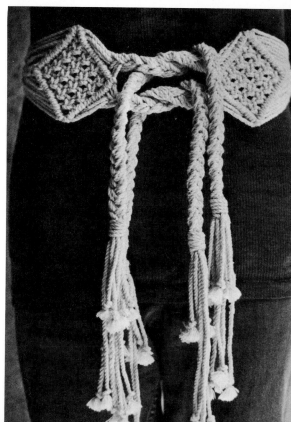

3

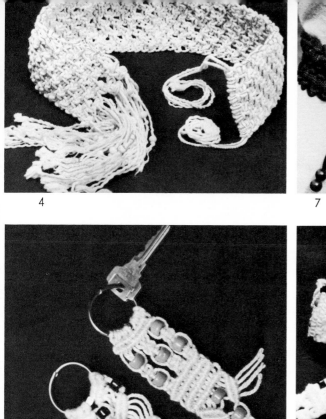

4

7

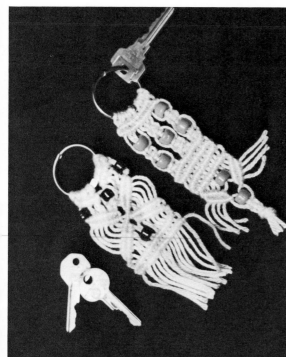

5

6

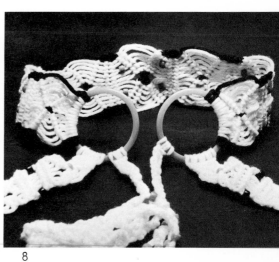

8

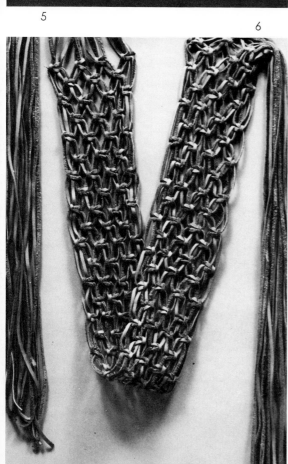

9

10

Beautifully designed necklaces attest to the pattern variety achieved by clever knotters. You can copy any of these designs easily by mounting cords and following the knots which you should be familiar with after only a few of the practice ties shown in Chapter 2. Use beads of your choice and cords that you have available in about a 1/16-inch or smaller diameter. The top left necklace uses 12 knotting strands of lightweight jute; the others, 16 strands of linen. (Top necklaces, Joyce Barnes; Bottom, Ruth Nensteil)

4 Jewelry— Delicate and Bold

Macramé jewelry is popular, pretty, and practical. The knotting goes quickly because the working cords are short. Knot patterns may be closely tied or contain many floating areas. Designs may be casual or dressy. Varied cords such as jute, heavy nylon, seine twine, navy cord, leather, and others result in gutsy, bold jewelry. Fine cords, including crochet cotton, linen warp, lightweight nylon, Swistraw, and gold and silver thread, yield delicate pieces that may be cherished for years.

The search for beads, bells, buttons, and handmade ceramic pieces that can be knotted into the work is part of the fun and beauty of jewelry making. Joyce Barnes is among the most inventive users of assorted found objects and handmade beads. Some of her neckware resembles intricately made assemblages mixed with knotting. They may include bells, pre-Columbian stone replicas, corks, pebbles, driftwood, feathers, leather, washers, and other items hard to recognize in their new context. Other knotters add antique beads, lengths of copper tubing cut to size, and objects culled from hardware stores and picked up on beaches. Holes may easily be drilled into seashells and tree fruits and nuts, and the pieces tied into Macramé.

To help string cords, use a thin piece of wire in the same way as a needle threader. Pull through with pliers if necessary. Beads that defy stringing can be attached with thin wire and wound inconspicuously into the work. Cord ends can be stiffened by dipping into melted paraffin or clear nail polish. Bead holes may be enlarged with a hand drill or rattail file.

There is no one best way to knot a necklace. For pieces that slip over the head, knotting may begin at the center back, and each side tied so that the knots match. The piece is joined in the center and the front panel is designed. Knotting may also begin at front bottom and worked to the top where both sides may be knotted together or joined by a fastening.

Styles that will fit close to the neck must be designed so they can be fastened at the back. Several closing methods are illustrated. Wire jewelry rings, available from craft and jewelry supply stores, may be used as the holding line and the cords mounted directly on the ring. A knotted braid or a cord line may be used so the length of the piece is adjustable when tied at the back.

Cord endings at the front of the jewelry must be carefully designed and finished. They are a perfect excuse for incorporating beads, for fringes, wrapping (see pages 87, 88), or unusual and interesting knot variations.

An easy way to measure cord for necklaces is to make a doubled cord as long as you are tall, or to your hemline or waistline, depending upon the desired length of the finished necklace. Wind the cord around your neck and hold with your foot or knee, then snip at one side and the doubled cords are ready to pin to the knotting surface.

A bib necklace with black and white wood beads is sporty and casual when made of white cotton seine twine mounted on a black rayon cord that ties in back. The same necklace design in nylon cord or silk rattail with glass beads could be very dressy and an important accessory to a simple basic dress. (Shirley Volpe)

To make the bib necklace of white cotton, you will need 1/16-inch seine twine: 26 cords five feet long (folded in half and mounted to yield 72 knotting strands each 2 1/2 feet long). Mount with Lark's Head on doubled black cord long enough to tie around neck comfortably, or use a holding line in color to contrast with the beads. Use approximately 30 round white beads and 22 black beads. Work one row of Square Knots. Make a second row of Alternating Square Knots and string a white bead on the anchor strands of each knot. Continue to tie eight rows of Alternating Square Knots. Make the knots in each row progressively larger so that collar will spread around the chest. String beads in the Square Knots to form an interesting pattern. The beads at the bottom row are held in place with two Overhand Knots. Trim the fringe while the necklace is on you and not on the knotting board so it will hang in a proper curve.

Dress. Andy Pawlan. ⅜-in. rayon cord. All Square Knots and Clove Hitches. Worked over a mannequin. *Below top.*

Tablecloth. Ruth Hofferth. White seine twine. *Below bottom.*

Hanging Plant Holder. Esther Parada. Jute. Knotting begins from plastic ring at bottom. Then cords are worked into a cylinder at top. *Right top.*

Waist Cincher Belt. Joan Michaels Paque. Yellow Jute-Tone. Clove Hitching worked as a woven motif. *Right bottom.* (Photo, Henry Paque)

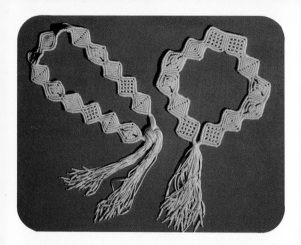

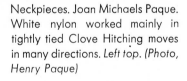

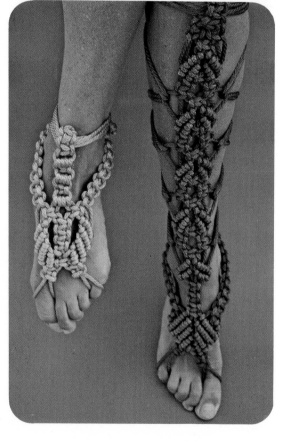

Neckpieces. Joan Michaels Paque. White nylon worked mainly in tightly tied Clove Hitching moves in many directions. *Left top.* *(Photo, Henry Paque)*

Knapsack. Joy Wulke. Combination crochet and Macramé with jute. *Left bottom.* *(Photo, Courtesy artist)*

Macramé Trim on a Suede Skirt. Susan Peters. Jute Clove Hitch chevron design pattern is used as trim by punching holes in suede and mounting jute directly to suede. *Right top.*

Barefoot Sandals. Corki Weeks. Dyed nylon braided cord uses knot loops to hook around toes. Same idea could be mounted between leather soles. *Right bottom.*

Knotted and Crocheted Skirt. Joan Michaels Paque and Mary Mulcahy. White cotton twine. Single, double, and triple crochet is used for the body of the skirt. A Macramé fringe is added to bottom crochet row and designed with alternating Overhand Knots. Crocheted belt with tassle is strung through open crochet stitches.

Body Covering. Joan Michaels Paque. Rug yarn. May be worn over a body stocking or with a pair of hip huggers. *Top.*

Green Bib. Sally Davidson. Silk rattail cord in all Square Knots. *Right. (Courtesy artist)*

Cape. Andy Pawlan. Braided nylon or rayon cord in white that you can dye is available in hardware stores or in colors from Macramé suppliers. Easy to make with all Alternating Square Knots and Clove Hitches. *Top.*

Vest. Bill Brewer. Natural jute with leather front panels. *Bottom.* (Photo, Lorraine Ohlson)

1. Macramé Lamp Covers. Joan Michaels Paque. Synthetic cord. *(Photo, Henry Paque)*

2. Room Divider. Estelle Carlson. Back panel of unknotted knitting worsted mounted on branch and held at bottom with another branch. Assymetrical white nylon knotting. Overhand knotted tassles have a small rock tied in for weighting.

3. Wind Chimes. Dona Meilach. Macra-Cord tied in Alternating Overhand Knots with long seashells tied on. Shell holes made with hand drill.

4. Trophy. Joan Michaels Paque. Animal's head is made completely of fibers with no armature. *(Photo, Henry Paque)*

5. Belt. Ursula MacPherson. White braided cord. Alternate Half Hitching with English buttons.

6. Neck Collar. Esther Parada. Variegated gold nylon cord is mounted with intricately knotted picots at center. Floating cords hang to waist.

2

1

3

4

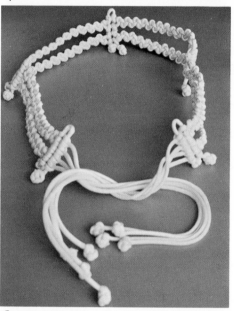

5

7

8

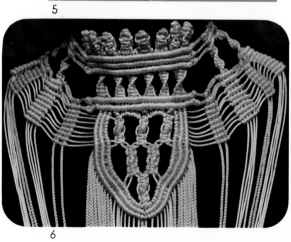

6

7. Suspenders. Joyce Barnes. Jute. Illustrates the carefully controlled use of color that can be accomplished with Macramé.

8. Necklace. Eileen Bernard. Gold and silver thread intricately worked with antique beads for a dressy and unusual piece of jewelry.

Neckpiece. Rosita Montgomery. Dull green cowhair, rug yarn, and replicas of Pre-Columbian stones. *Left top. (Photo, courtesy artist)*

Midi Skirt. Andy Pawlan. A ⅜-in. rayon braided cord with Square Knots, Clove Hitches, and a panel of Josephine Knots at knees. *Right top.*

Vest. Andy Pawlan. Front and back view showing increase for shaping with white cord worked into a panel of Josephine Knots. *Bottom.*

Necklaces of Alternating Square Knots loosely tied result in a flowerlike design when you use about a 1/16-inch Polyolefin Macramé cord (No. 4 Pacific Cordage Co.). One row of Clove Hitches following a Lark's Head mount prevents the necklace from spreading and helps it to hold its shape.

Top necklace: Use 16 cords eight feet long to yield 32 knotting strands. Mount on a cord adding a crow bead between each mounting. Continue in pattern. For the neckband, use six cords (12 strands) about five feet long added with Lark's Head to one side of neckpiece, then working in pattern. When the desired length for the neckband is reached, Clove Hitch the ends tightly to the original mounting on the other side, work the loose ends under, and add a dab of glue to hold if necessary. (Stiff cords often hold without gluing.)

Bottom necklaces: (Left) Mount 12 three-yard lengths of cord directly on the neck ring for 24 knotting cords. (Right) Mount 14 three-yard lengths for 28 knotting cords. Work two rows of Clove Hitches, then Alternating Square Knots to the length desired. Add beads on the anchor cords of the Square Knots as in the patterns shown or your own designs. Finish the ends with feathers or beads. Feathers may require wrapping and gluing or they may be secured by pushing feather end into a bead strung at the bottom of the cords. (Eileen Bernard)

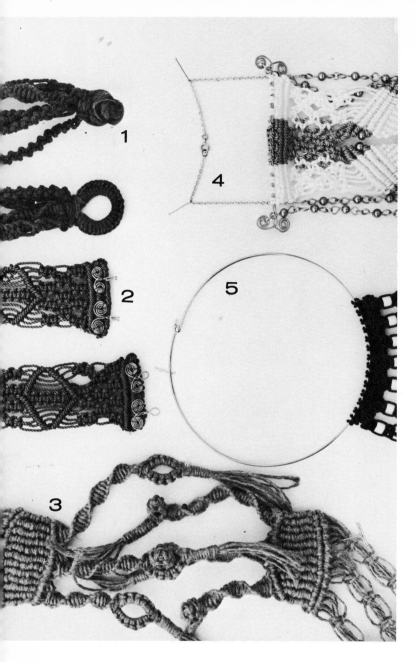

FASTENING IDEAS: When you wish to have neckwear meet at the back rather than go over the head, you can use several methods shown here:

1. A bead at one end is laced on a cord before the cord is knotted into the work. The "hole" on the other end is made by Clove Hitching one cord around all the others until the required length is reached, then all ends progress into the knotting.

2. Metal hooks and eyes may be sewn to the inside hem of the finished pieces. Velcro zipper lengths may be stitched or glued to the hems.

3. Separated sennits of Square Knots form the hole for the Square Knot buttons made at end of neck chain.

4. A gold jewelry chain is added to a handmade brass rod holding line.

5. The necklace ring is available in gold or silver finish.

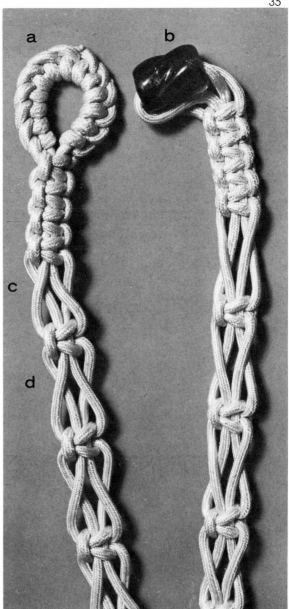

Left: White silk braided necklace with red and blue beads. The necklace is begun from doubled cords at the clasp end, and the chain is tied with a variation of the Square Knot (see detail right). Begin with two three-yard cords doubled at each side for four working strands and knot lengths of chain in Square Knot variations. When the cords meet at the center front add beads. Beneath beads use the left end cord for an anchor, and four additional 36-inch lengths of cords (eight knotting strands) are Clove Hitched to result in a total of 16 knotting strands. Continue in pattern adding beads as shown. (Susann Craig)

Right: Detail of clasp end and Square Knot variation (left). To begin hole of clasp, (a) double cords; pin three doubled portions to knotting board and use one cord to Clove Hitch over all. Then bring four cords down and work in four Square Knots.

For bead end (b), string bead at doubled portion and allow slack so bead can push through the hole. Tie four Square Knots.

Square Knot variation for neckband (c), pick up the two center anchor strands and reverse their position, now using them for knotting strands. (d) Reverse the order again, so the procedure consists of picking up the former anchor and tying over the preceding knotting cords. The pattern will remain consistent if you always pick up the anchors from under the knotting cords. (Susann Craig)

 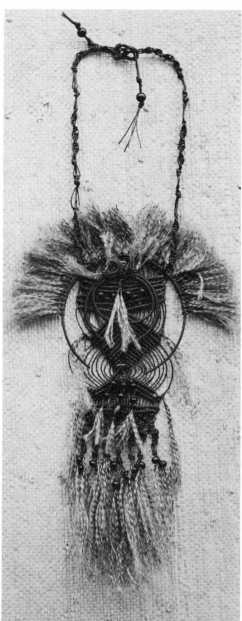

Left: Large necklace of yellow navy cord buttons at the back. Neck chain is a mixture of Half Knot Twists and grouped Overhand Knots. Ends of the chain become the holding line for new cords which are mounted with the Lark's Head. Straight and diagonal Clove Hitched bars are combined with floating cords and Square Knot Buttons (page 90). Wrapping unifies the cords and a silver star from an old earring is mounted in the top center. (Berni Gorski)

Right: A neckpiece with a very primitive feeling is achieved by fraying the ends of dark brown elm flax which has a beautiful silky, fluffy feeling. Several wire circles are used both as a holding line for mounted cords and as decorative motifs tied in with the knotting. Black wooden beads contribute to the success of the total design. (Berni Gorski; Photos, Henry Gorski)

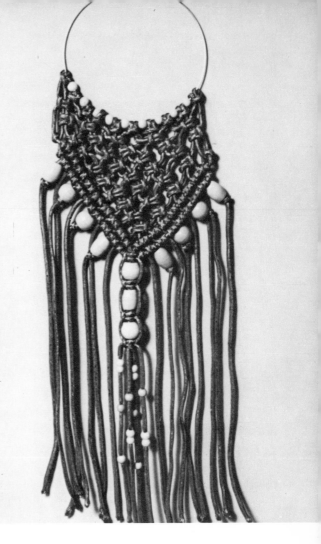

Bib necklace of blue silk braid about 3/32-inch diameter with imported green and yellow glass beads. Mount ten six-foot cords (= 20 three-foot strands) on a jewelry ring with a bead between each cord. Work three rows of tightly tied Alternating Square Knots, then begin to decrease and shape the edge using two rows of Clove Hitches, but continuing the Alternating Square Knots into the V pattern. Add the beads as shown and hold in place with an Overhand Knot. (Susann Craig)

Necklace of red rattail with black beads from India and turquoise donkey beads. An old bracelet forms the central circle from which the scallops are extended. The circle is simply tied with the Clove Hitch as though it were a holding line. Dampen the rattail cord slightly with a moist sponge when working to prevent knots from slipping out. As the cord dries, the knots hold tightly. (Susann Craig)

A unique method of mounting cords is a variation of picots. Chenille yarn is Clove Hitched to the holding line, then the loose ends are strung through buttons and wrapped with another color cord. Buttons are strung on Square Knotting cords in the body of the necklace, and long seashells dangle at the ends. The dark cords between are simply doubled floating cords with a few beads. (Stana Coleman)

Very simple knotting is combined with copper-color hardware store washers and blanks from copper enameling jewelry. Black Macra-Cord and black beads complement the copper tones. (Stana Coleman)

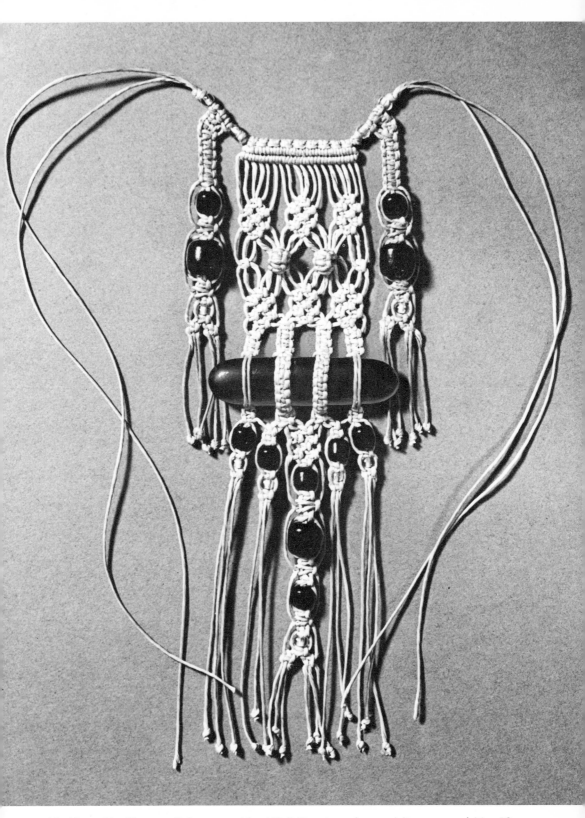

Necklace, Hip Flopper, G-String, or Mini Wall Hanging of waxed linen natural No. 12 cord with black wooden beads, clear beads, and a long black stone. Clove Hitches, Alternating Square Knots, Square Knot Buttons, and Overhand Knots. (Gerald Hodge; Photo, S. C. Whalen)

1

4

3

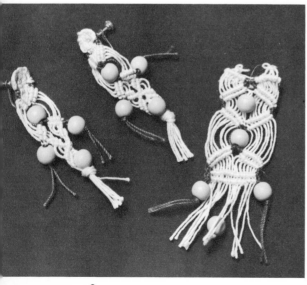

2

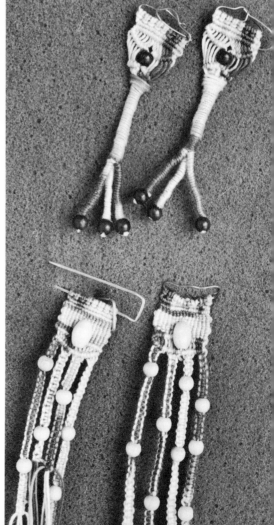

5

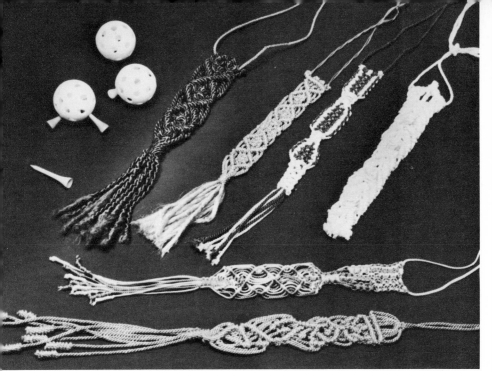

Lightweight soft cords most appropriate for earrings and matching neckwear are varieties of crochet cord, navy cord, yarn, and cotton and nylon twine. Earring backs for pierced ears, and fake pierced and screw backings are available from jewelry findings and craft companies. Work the earrings from the bottom of a U-shaped pin stuck into your knotting surface. Then thread a wire or cord through the Lark's Head mount, remove the U pin, and attach to the finding. Pin backings may be stitched, tied, or glued to finished jewelry.

8

1. Neckware and matching earring in blue and green linen cord with imported wood and bamboo beads available at craft and import shops. (Shirley Volpe)

2. Earrings and matching pin of pink and blue crochet cotton with beads. (Jeanette Cohen)

3. Pin of black and white Lily Macra-Cord made with the Josephine Knot (page 90). Ends are cut and glued. (Sally Davidson)

4. Simple-to-make earrings of one ten-inch length of Lily Macra-Cord folded in half with a bead added. Knotting is six Alternating Half Hitches. Ends are fringed. Finding is attached by piercing into or wiring onto a loop of cord. (Dona Meilach)

5. Earrings of variegated Coats and Clark's crochet cotton. They are intricately knotted, some have long wrapping. (Al Meilach)

6. Men's ties of different cords and knot variations. A male version of simple-to-make neckware. (Stewart Purinton)

7. Man's jewelry is a sennit of Square Knots with a copper washer, wood ball, and wrapped leather tubes. (Joyce Barnes)

8. Man's tie of Josephine Knots (page 90) of rawhide. Rawhide should be run under water after knotting, then smoothed. It will dry and hold knots as shaped. (Dona Meilach)

MORE MOTIFS FOR JEWELRY

As you become adept at following directions for jewelry and reading what is happening with knots, the real challenge is in combining motifs and changing patterns into new designs. Therefore the details shown may be used, combined, added to, and subtracted, much as the letters of the alphabet are rearranged to make many words.

1. For a different ending from straight fringe and beads, tie Alternating Half Hitch chains held at the end with beads and used in conjunction with unknotted cord. (Joyce Barnes)

2. A wood ring Clove Hitched to the work for design and texture. Also use parts of bones from round-steak. (Shirley Volpe)

3. Square Knot sennits crossed over may be of one or more colors. (Ruth Nensteil)

4. Groups of cords and a strand of leather are added to a cord which has been doubled back through strung beads. Cord is an added anchor length from Clove Hitch Bars. The cord group is decorative and functional as it prevents the anchor cord from slipping up through the bead. (Joyce Barnes)

5. Cords knotted within cords and strung with beads. (Joyce Barnes)

6. Multiples of Half Knot Twists and Square Knotted sennits of different cords may be combined for a rich, textural interest. (Joyce Barnes)

7. Tiny feathers and small beads are combined with fine linen cord in tight, perfectly tied Horizontal Clove Hitches. (Annabel Bergstrom)

8. Mix and divide the knotting cords for Square Knot sennits and Half Knot Twists; then hang an almond shell and a bell in the center. (Joyce Barnes)

1

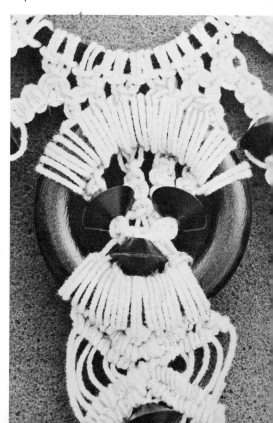

2

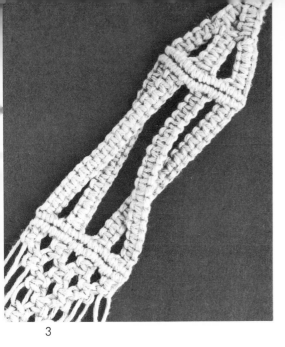

3

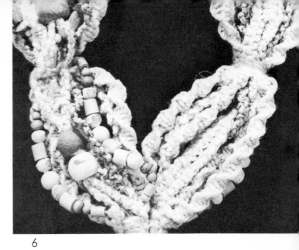

6

4

5

7

8

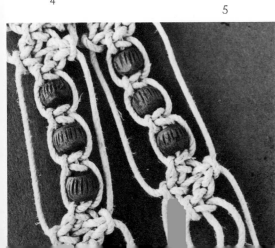

Macramé headwear has many personalities, from airy, flimsy, coquettish styles for women to those inspired by a gaucho hat for men. You can make bun holders and scarf styles with cascading cords for a modern young lady to hold her flying tresses.

After you try the hatmaking methods illustrated, design your own headgear as wild or as simple as you like. Create your favorite hat styles by knotting over a favorite old hat. Either stuff the original hat or put it on a wig stand and work directly over it if you don't mind a few pinholes. Or shape several layers of Styrofoam built up to the necessary crown height and work your hat over that.

Hats may be started from a plastic or rubber ring pinned into a foam wig stand (page 9) as Eileen Bernard does. Stewart Purinton begins from a center flat oval or a group of cords and then moves them to a wood or foam wig stand shape to knot the crown and brim.

Loosely knotted patterns should be of fairly stiff cords. For closely knotted designs, the knots themselves will hold the hat in shape. Brims that tend to flop may be tacked with needle and thread, or thin wire may be inserted through the knots to help the brims hold their shape. Sometimes a few coats of spray starch will help. The hats may be blocked by steaming depending upon the cord used.

Hats may be made open and airy or tightly knotted for a closed design. Appearance will vary greatly depending upon the colors and combinations of cords. (Eileen Bernard)

Cloche hat styles (left and above) are made of Polyolefin Macramé cord (Pacific Cordage) that is thin, yet stiff and holds a knot well. (Eileen Bernard)

General instructions for making cloche style hats:

Begin from a rubber washer or plastic cabone ring (found at drapery counters) pinned at back top of a Styrofoam wig stand. Mount with 28 three-yard cords, each folded in half. If the cords are too numerous for mounting on a small ring, increase in the Square Knots in the third row to expand the circular size. (See page 63 for Square Knot increasing.) Continue the Alternating Square Knot pattern using one or more Square Knot sennits per row, until the crown is the desired length.

Pin a length of round elastic thread, allowing very little stretch, at base of crown and tie. Clove Hitch all cords around the elastic. Between the knotted cords, and in the spaces remaining on the band, increase by Clove Hitching an additional 14 one-yard doubled lengths evenly spaced all around. Work the remainder of brim. Make a separate Square Knot sennit to cover the elastic band as in the hat on left. Or lace with ribbon as above. Place the hat on a wig stand, dampen slightly, shape, and dry. (Eileen Bernard)

Gaucho hat of gold and white nylon twist seine twine is cool, airy, and different. (Stewart Purinton)

To make the gaucho hat, you will need approximately 112 yards of No. 36 seine twine nylon twist or a similar cord of one or two colors as desired. 7 3/4- to 8-inch head size. Crown is three inches high, brim is three inches wide.

Cord lengths required:

36 cords six feet long (divided into two colors).
16 short white cords about six inches long for spacing at top.
28 cords 2 1/2 feet long for increase at the top of the crown.
One holding cord five feet long to be doubled and used for center beginning and first top edge.
Three anchor cords each four feet long for base of crown and brim edge.

Work the top of the crown on a knotting board but pin an oval paper shape cut to size of crown under the knotting. For the riser part of the crown, work over Styrofoam or cardboard ovals cut to the shape and height of crown desired.

Top of Crown *(see detail A)*

Place a doubled holding line along the center of the oval and mount 36 six-foot cords using a Clove Hitch. Separate the cords so there are equal numbers of strands on each side of the holding line.

Now, to create airiness and prevent cords from sliding along holding line, use the 16 short spacing cords six inches long and Clove Hitch them along the holding line between each group of four knotting cords. Knot tightly and clip underneath.

Follow the pattern for knotting as shown in Detail A so it fits within the paper oval. When you knot to the edge of the oval, pin an extra length of central holding line around the ends and Clove Hitch cords around. But as you work add two cords between each Square Knot group. These are your twenty-eight 2 1/2 foot cords which are doubled and Clove Hitched in the alternating color arrangement. Color placement need not be exact as strands move in and out during knotting.

Crown and Brim *(see detail B)*

Make Alternating Square Knot pattern down the side, working around layers of cardboard or Styrofoam in this progression of 3, 1, 2, 1, 2, 1, 2, for seven rows (less for a shorter crown). At the base of the riser pin a new anchor cord all around and Clove Hitch all cords. Place the hat on the working surface and draw an oval for brim shape and size, and work in single Alternating Square Knots all around, tying knots more loosely as you work out to the edge. At center front and center rear, in third row of knotting, tie the knots more loosely to help relieve oval pull. If necessary increase the Square Knots as shown (page 63).

Edge of Brim

Add the two remaining anchor cords around the edge and Clove Hitch over the cords. Tie very tightly. Trim the edge close.

Finishing

If the hat needs minor shaping, dampen and pull to shape. To keep the brim up, tack the side edge to the crown, and add wire or spray starch for desired shape and stiffness.

Detail A of top of crown.

Detail B of crown and brim. Note progression of knot numbers before rows alternate.

Ladies' hats are made using different approaches from the gaucho hat on the previous page. The hat at left is light blue nylon. It begins as shown in Details A and B below: lay out an oval on the knotting board and place a thin dowel or knitting needle across the center as shown and tie Alternating Square Knots to fill the oval. Then Clove Hitch bars at outline of shape. Mount the crown on top of a wig stand and continue knotting, adding cords uniformly as needed.

The hat at right is of black and royal blue nylon twist. It begins from a group of cords at the top, then is knotted in an Alternating Square Knot pattern until the shape expands. Cords are increased in the Square Knots (see page 63). As the knotting progresses, the work is placed on a wig stand or old hat stuffed to shape, then knotted.

Detail A

Detail B

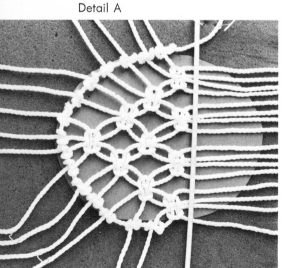

Macramé headdress begins from a napkin ring which fits on top of the head and is used to pull the hair into a pony tail and then cascade down back. Shells at the ends of the cords tinkle as the wearer moves. (Josephine E. Diggs; Photo, artist)

Juliet cap or bun holder may be worn by women or little girls. Made completely of widely spaced Alternating Square Knots, the cap begins from a plastic ring at the center back. (Virginia Black; Photo, artist)

Head veil made of rows of Half Knot Twists alternated every ten knots in the same way as the Alternating Square Knots. This keeps the rows intertwined and shaped. Forty-three ten-foot cords (96 five-foot strands) are mounted on a wrapped doubled cord sewn to a two-inch length of elastic at the back to make the veil fit around the head. Stonewear beads on back are held with Overhand Knots. (Louise Todd; Photo, artist)

Jute purses are basically the same, using variations of cords, flap, and handle designs. However, only the purse, top right, is completely knotted; the other two have crocheted pouches with knotted flaps. Crochet and Macramé are natural companions when handled cleverly. (Lois Constantine)

6 Handbags

Handbags, dressy and casual, small and large, may be knotted for every occasion from beach to formal wear. Despite the variety of styles illustrated, it must be emphasized that all are made from two easy approaches. The handbags illustrated at left are made as one long rectangular shape, then the sides knotted together and the flap allowed to hang over. Straps are added.

The other approach is to work around a tubular shape or framework so no side seams are necessary. Ends that result at the bottom of some bags may remain as a fringe or they may be brought to the inside of the bag, tied tightly, and clipped short. A dab of glue will hold the ends and the lining will conceal raw edges. Pouch parts may also be made separately, then new cords mounted for the flap and for a bottom fringe if desired.

It is easy to adapt any of the styles shown to either method depending upon how you prefer to work. Your major decisions will be the style, size of bag, color, and cord. Textured cords such as jute, manilla, and hemp are more adaptable to casual styles but can be worked into dressy bags also. Nylon, silk, rayon, and other shiny surface cords are perfect for dressier bags. Purse cords should be carefully pretested for color fastness so the color doesn't come off when hands or clothes are moist.

Purse handles and other findings can be taken from old purses, purchased from Macramé suppliers, craft shops, leather goods manufacturers, and knotting shops. Many of the findings can also be improvised from hardware store and drapery counter sources including wood and metal rings, beads, brass rods, and anything you can imagine.

Purses usually are lined, especially if the knot patterns are not tightly designed, to prevent objects from poking through them. Select lining fabrics that match or contrast with the purse. Make them into a pouch shape slightly smaller than the purse to prevent the purse from stretching out. Add an extra inside pocket to the lining. Turn under the top edge and machine stitch, then hand tack the lining to the inside of the purse.

Using the same methods of purse making, fashion eyeglass cases, herb pouches, and beach bags. You can make them for youngsters, too.

a

b

General instructions for purses:

When pouches and flaps are made as one long rectangle, the sides are laced together. To lace, add two doubled cords and crossover between the edges of each side. The sides may be joined with only crisscrossing cords or they may be Square Knotted as they are laced, making a wider side panel for easier accessibility into the purse.

Purse A:

For combination crochet and Macramé bags you will need about 2 1/2 large balls of jute from the hardware store or four four-ounce tubes (75 yards per tube) Lily Jute-Tone, a size K aluminum crochet hook, and wooden beads for trim. For the size of purse shown, eight inches square, make your first crochet chain 24 stitches. Start the second row by going into the second chain from the end. Double crochet across each row. At the end of each row, chain two single chains before starting back again. Make 22 to 24 rows for front and back depending upon length of purse desired. Some people prefer to make two separate pieces, each 12 rows, then join them on the bottom and sides.

For the crochet handle, use two or three rows of single or double crochet the length of handle you want.

Add Macramé flap by mounting Lark's Head directly at the top back edge of crochet, then tie the knotting in the pattern desired.

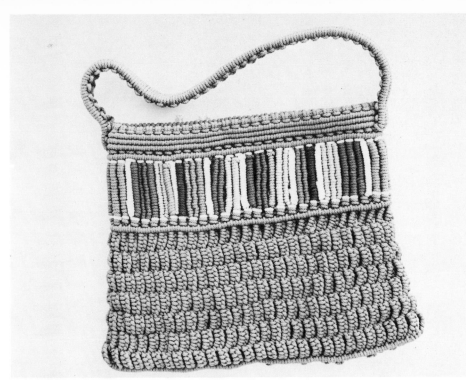

This handbag knotted in the round has unusual features. A band of colored cords is made by wrapping additional cords around vertical strands as they are brought down in the pattern. Only the original gold-colored cords are knotted in with Vertical Clove Hitches. The repeat curving pattern is created by straightening the Clove Hitch twisting chain (page 92). A zipper is added to the lining for closing. Horizontal Clove Hitch Bars at the base help the purse to retain its shape. Made of Lily Jute-Tone. (Joyce Barnes)

Purse B:

For a knotted pouch you will need the same amount of material as above. Begin at top inside front and knot a rectangle in the pattern desired. Where folds will occur at the bottom front and back at the top flap, tie a Clove Hitch Bar for better shaping. The flap is a continuation of pouch knotting. With Alternating Square Knots use beads and an edging of curved Clove Hitch Bars. The handle is attached with metal rings and combines Square Knotting and Wrapping. (Lois Constantine)

A special twining board used by weavers is improvised for knotting in round tubular shapes, but you can use leftover spindles from drapery trim or make your own setup over a chair or around two dowels screwed into a flat board.

1

1. The gold nylon bag is made in two parts and knotted together at the sides. The doubled lining has a zipper closing. Knotting begins from brass rods fitted with brass beads. Glass gold beads knotted within for a fantastic appearance in a prize-winning design for the artist. (Eileen Bernard)

2. Jute can be dressy when made into a small, simple, and daintily knotted handbag. Wood handles are covered with cords Clove Hitched around them. (Lynn Needham)

3. Small purses can be designed for many purposes. Top: Evil Eye herbal pouch of tan navy cord has a bead painted with the evil eye. Herbs, placed in a piece of nylon stocking, are easily changed (Winkie Fordney). Bottom: Eyeglass case attached to a band of leather for a holding line. (Jeanette Cohen)

4. A Macramé fringe added to a purse and many other accessories such as a skirt, pillows, and jackets, change their appearance. (Stana Coleman)

5. Left: Eggshell nylon purse is basically the same knotted pouch style with knotted flap as the jute purses on page 52. But the material and slightly smaller size give it a dressy, delicate appearance. Right: Cotton seine twine zipper top purse has a crocheted pouch, Macramé bottom and fringe. (Lois Constantine)

6. White nylon bag knotted from rings with Clove Hitching. Braided and wrapped handle is used to simulate a drawstring style. (Mary Baughn)

2

3

5

4

6

Gold vest of rug yarn may be worn by a man or woman. See instructions and back view on page 58. Rug yarn is thick, so the knotting goes quickly and the knot patterns stand out. Cord is soft, making the finished piece easy to wear, mobile, and washable. (Eileen Bernard)

7

Body Coverings

Practical and offbeat body coverings are sure to be conversation pieces. Some of the styles illustrated are for men and women and may be adapted to children too.

Cords used for body coverings should be selected with care so they will wear well and not stretch out of shape. Cotton, silk, rayon, nylon cord, seine twine, knitting yarn, cable cord, rug yarn, rattail, and weaving cords are preferred. Try to adapt the cords to the style; thick cords knotted are sometimes too heavy and bulky to wear; jutes and other fuzzy hard cords can irritate the skin; stiff cords do not move well with the wearer.

To assure proper fit, there are three basic ways to approach a clothing item: (1) knot a sample of the cord for a size gauge as mentioned in Chapter 1. For a chest size, for example, count how many mounted cords equal one inch, then multiply the number of cords in one inch by the number of inches needed. (2) Make a paper pattern of the exact shape to be designed, then place the pattern on a large knotting board of soft wood or Celotex and fill in this pattern as you knot, increasing and decreasing for the neck and armholes, and shaping the bust and waist as necessary. (3) Work over a dressmaker dummy, Styrofoam form, or pillow tied into shape; then you can pin the knots directly into the form to keep them even as you work.

Buy patterns from recognized pattern books *(Vogue, McCall's, Butterick, Simplicity)* and adapt to knotting by pinning the pattern parts over a mannequin or to your knotting board. Convert carefully so you don't include seam allowances if none are required. Depending upon size and adaptation, garments may be knotted all around or in separate panels which may then be knotted or laced together.

The biggest problem in making accessories is estimating the amount of cord required, and this can be done best by tying the sample gauge mentioned. If you dye cords, dye the entire amount required in one dye lot, always overestimating the cord requirements. The same is true when purchasing colored cords. If you're not sure of color fastness and shrinkage, pretest the knotted gauge. Draw the gauge size on a piece of paper, wash the gauge and let it dry, then place it on drawing. Estimate the shrinkage, if any, and allow for shrinkage in knotting unless the cord can be reblocked to shape. When in doubt, have the finished pieces dry-cleaned.

Back view of gold vest
(page 56) by Eileen Bernard.

*The gold vest is one rectangular panel made by attaching the required number
of knotting cords to a straight holding line which fits around chest measurement.
Braid three 72-inch cords for a holding line for extra strength and to reduce
stretchability. Then, depending upon the gauge and size required (140 cords
were used for this vest), mount the cords with a Lark's Head. Remember to
mount a number of cords divisible by four so the Square Knot pattern will
work out evenly. Estimate the length by measuring from the top of the chest
to the finished length desired, then multiply by eight. You will use doubled cords.*

*Always Horizontal Clove Hitch the first row to reduce stretch further,
then work in pattern until you reach finished length desired allowing lengths
for fringe and beads.*

*For straps, cut 16 cords (32 strands) about three yards long. Double
and attach eight cords to each side of the back of the original braided holding
line with a Lark's Head. Knot in pattern to length required, then Clove Hitch
to the front. String beads on loose ends. Block, if necessary, as you would
block a knitted garment.*

Man's Vest of 1/8-inch-gauge manila and jute twine. (Berni Gorski)

Cut newspaper patterns for two fronts and a back. Pin or trace the pattern outline onto the knotting board. The three pieces were worked separately of 1/8-inch manila rope for fronts and back. For underarm, Alternating Half Hitch pattern jute twine was used. Extra strong polished India twine doubled is the holding cord for the neckline and armholes. Pin the holding cord to the board along the neckline and armhole pattern edge, then mount the cords with a Lark's Head and work into the pattern as shown. Lace the sides together at the armholes. Lace two cords (four strands) into the edges and tie a Square Knot between each lacing all the way down to match the length of the panels. Unravel all end cords for extra full fringing. (Photo, Henry Gorski)

MINI AND OTHER LENGTH SKIRTS

*An outstanding skirt made of thick wool or synthetic cords can be made
very quickly. After mounting the knotting cords to the drawstring waistband,
the skirt is tied over a chair back or mannequin so it is a completely tubular
knotted piece with no seams. The finished length is 15 inches with fringe.
You can dye cords and mix colors using ecru, maroon, navy, and purple as
shown, other color combinations, or all one color. This piece is measured to
fit a 36-inch hip measurement, but because the knotted cords are very stretchy,
it will fit anyone with hips an inch or two smaller or larger. For other hip
sizes, adjust the mounted number of cords accordingly.*

*Use 320 yards of 3/8-inch-diameter braided silk, rayon, or polypropylene
cord. You will need 52 cords, each six yards long. Double (but do not use a
Lark's Head) onto four 40-inch strands used for the waistband. (Detail A)*

*Beginning at the point where the waistband cords meet, tie a row of
Square Knots with 4 cord multiples all around. Tie 18 rows (more or less
depending on your height) of Alternating Square Knots, allowing about a
1/2-inch space between each row, to begin the hem pattern (Detail B), divide
cards into groups of 16. Beginning at the center front, tie Diagonal Clove Hitch
Bars as shown. Under the peak of the diagonal tie two Square Knots with four
center cords, then a row of Square Knots along bottom. Repeat the pattern evenly
all around. Unravel the ends and apply dabs of Elmer's Glue or fabric glue to
the back of each Square Knot to hold securely.*

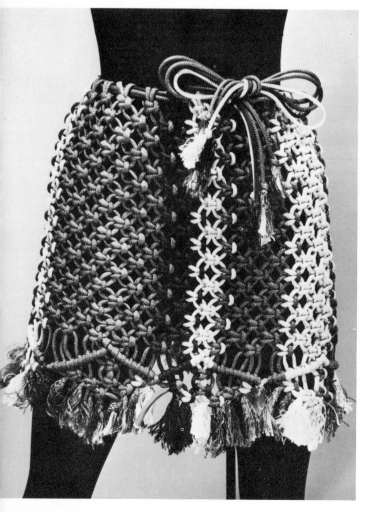

Drawstring skirt is made of four
colors that give a striped effect
when worked mainly in Alternating Square Knots. (Andy Pawlan)

Detail A. Waistband mounting detail for miniskirt showing how cords are used to square knot first row and then alternating square knots.

Detail B. Hem design detail for miniskirt using Diagonal Clove Hitches with Square Knots.

For the midiskirt illustrated in the color section use this beginning at waistband consisting of two sets of three rows Clove Hitched to assure a fit that molds to the shape. Measure the hips, estimate and cut the number of cords needed into 12-yard lengths. Double and mount on the waistband cord. Work Alternating Square Knots to about one inch above the knees, then continue in pattern of Clove Hitches, Josephine Knots (page 90), Square Knots, and floating cords.

To finish at the hem, bring each loose cord back under a knot on the inside, cut the cord close, and secure with a dab of glue.

Pullover of twisted 3/8-inch-diameter nylon cord in three colors. The shirt begins from four cords at the shoulder tied in Alternating Square Knots, then knots are increased at the neckline and armhole as shown at right. Work over a paper pattern from the shoulders down in front and back until the armhole bottoms are reached, then work over a chair or around a knotting board for a continuous tubular shape. Or the piece may be worked as a front and back panel, then laced at the sides. (Andy Pawlan)

Mini pullover made as above in a shortie style. If you need additional width at the bust or waist, add cords unobtrusively using the Square Knot increase as shown at right. (Andy Pawlan)

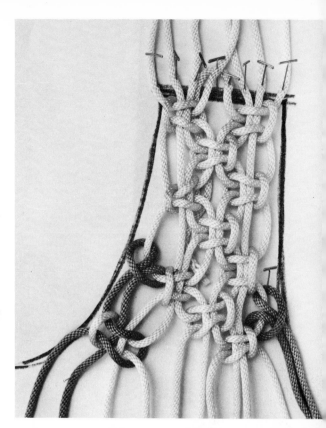

SQUARE KNOT INCREASING

To increase at edge with Square Knots mount cords at top shoulder and pin over the pattern. As the neck and armholes require shaping, add a doubled cord and place it through the loop of the previously tied Square Knot with a Lark's Head; then work it into the Alternating Square Knot pattern. Always remember that multiples must be added in amounts of four knotting strands so that the Square Knot pattern works out correctly.

Square Knot increase within the work: To increase within a Square Knot pattern, place a doubled cord between the loops of the previous two Square Knots in the loops they have formed. Always add two cords (four knotting strands), one at each side of a Square Knot so the number of strands fits into the pattern unobtrusively.

For another Square Knot increase method, see page 89.

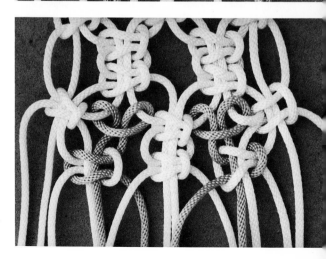

When new cords are properly added in the Square Knotting, they won't show, but the pattern will be enlarged.

Body covering with a high neck that buttons at one side was inspired by neckwear shown on bronze heads from Benin, Bini Tribe, Nigeria, dating from about 1550. Clothing and artwork from primitive cultures illustrated in art books and exhibited in natural history museums are a natural stimulation for original Macramé designs. Front view (above), back view (left). (Andy Pawlan)

Bodice knotted completely in silk rattail cord starts from the center of the breast with four cords mounted over a circular cord pinned to the board, then pulled tight to close the circle. Cords are easily added as needed by increasing within and around the Clove Hitching and in Square Knotting. Approximately 100 yards of cord were used. (Henry Majinn; Photo, Leo Sturman)

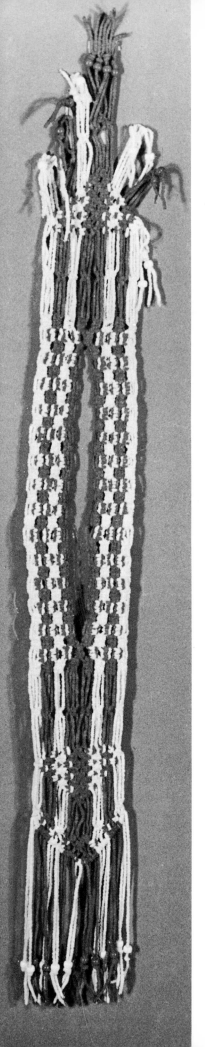

PONCHOS — PERT, PRETTY, PRACTICAL

Ponchos are popular in a variety of widths and lengths for men and women. The principle is to knot a rectangular design, but leave an open slit for the head simply by working the knots as two separate strips. After the desired head hole size is made (be sure it's big enough to slip over easily after it's closed) bring the cords together again. Ponchos may be knotted from the shoulders down to the front and to the back, so working cords are not as cumbersome as if the piece were tied from one end to the other.

 The fit of ponchos is not so important, as they are usually made to hang loosely. You can begin to knot without worrying too much about gauge. For extra shaping at the neckline, draw a pattern on your knotting board and expand at the shoulder simply by casting on extra Square Knots, or adding in anchor cords and new knotting cords (see page 89 and index for increasing methods). To decrease an area, knot two cords together until you have the number of cords required for a certain width.

Left: Poncho of red and white Lily chenille yarn of about 3/32-inch diameter. Finished size, 60 inches long by 10 inches wide. Begin with 32 cords, 16 of each color, about 13 yards long. Mount in this progression: 2W, 2R, 2W, 4R, 2W, 2R, 2W. Begin knotting at the shoulders in Alternating Square Knots. Pin the cords to the board but do not mount on a holding line. Note in photo below, showing how a poncho is worn, that one end is tapered, the other squared off. (Julia Littell)

Reversible side.

Reversible brown and white poncho of Lily chenille yarn at a finished length of 45 inches with fringe; width, 15 inches. Measure the length desired from neck to hem and multiply by eight. You will need 56 cords (half of each color). Cords are most easily tied by mounting centers of cord at the shoulders, using a Clove Hitch Bar—then working down in two directions for front and back. Use one knotting strand as an anchor at each side of the neck opening and begin by Clove Hitching seven rows, then with Alternating Square Knots work a rounded neck opening with scallops at the outside shoulders. Work the knots loose and tight and spread the sections so they round out. The color panels have been reversed in front and back, so the brown stripe is in the center on one side, the white is on the other. Beads are strung at the ends. (Julia Littell)

Caftan of green linen has a Macramé poncho-neckpiece trim of white and blue Mexican yarn worked with flat and raised areas of knotting trimmed with glass beads. (Macramé, Lorraine Ohlson; caftan and photo, Florence B. Johnson)

White poncho (left) of assorted 5/16- and 3/8-inch cotton cable cord may be worn by a man or woman. Green and yellow poncho (right) of Bucilla Kraftwist cord used for rugs and heavy crochet work. Note how the colors move about in the piece. (Both ponchos by Jane A. Moody)

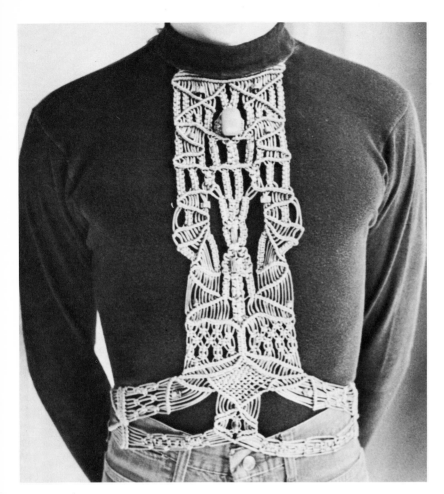

Male chest plate utilizes approximately 90 yards of rattail cord strung with African beads. The piece ties at the back of the neck. It is worked from the neck down in Square Knots and Clove Hitches with a woven panel at bottom center. Added cords extend out for the belt wrap. (Hildyne Manpearl; Photo, artist)

Crocheted cape-style poncho in progress. The body of the cape is crocheted and cords are added with Lark's Heads for a Macramé fringe. Bundles are a good method for preventing cords from tangling as you knot. (Lois Constantine; Photo, Virginia Black)

This white nylon body drape may be knotted long and worn over floor-length clothes. It may be adapted to shorter items or used only as a chest covering. The waistband at the sides is brought up around the back to brass rings as shown in the rear view of body drape (right). Mrs. Weeks works her body pieces over a dressmaker's dummy. (Corki Weeks; Photo, artist)

Wine and lavender rug filler yarn makes a smashing poncho with Josephine Knots tied in the center of Clove Hitch diamonds over each breast. (Note the grouping of long cords at the center, short cords at the sides, and shorter cords at the shoulders.) The back may be tied to full length as in front or made into a short collar with hanging fringe. Cords are mounted on the holding line with a single picot (page 93) for added detailing. Clove Hitch over new anchor cord at the waist to serve as belt and hold covering close to the body. (Sally Davidson)

Macramé is combined with card weaving in this body collar adapted from a design of ancient armor. All flat areas are woven on cardboard shapes. The Square Knot buttons in the center are combined with Clove Hitched bars. The entire outer edge is Clove Hitched. Wrapping at ends with tiny bells attached. Material is Lily Jute-Tone. (Libby Platus; Photo, Virginia Black)

Collar of green cotton crochet cord may be buttoned at front or back. It begins from a Lark's Head mount at the neck and is then expanded to lie flat over the shoulders. Cords are increased by adding over Clove Hitch Bars, always retaining a number of cords divisible by four so Square Knots and Half Knot Twists will work out evenly. (Esther Robinson)

Victorian choker collar is made by knotting 48 cords (96 strands) of No. 30 cotton seine twine from an anchor cord which will tie at back of neck. The first row of Clove Hitches is knotted over a second anchor cord which also ties at the back. Patterns of six rows of Alternating Square Knots tied closely are finished at the bottom with another row of Clove Hitches. Cords are unraveled for fringe and tied with Overhand Knots. Buttons are sewn at back top and bottom so the collar holds tightly on neck. (Sandra Harrison)

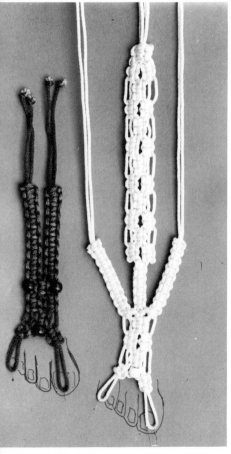

Barefoot sandals are tied with 1/8-inch nylon braid in ankle-strap and knee-high lacing styles using only the Square Knot and a few beads. They are quick and easy to make following the structure shown in the photo left. Work from toe to top directly from loops of doubled cord. (Do not mount with a Lark's Head.) Pin two loops of each doubled cord to fit around the first and fourth toes before knotting. For both sandals, only six cords are used. For the high laced sandal, the center sennit of Square Knots separates at the ankle into two sennits of Alternating Square Knots tied over only one anchor cord instead of the usual two. (Corki Weeks)

73

Shutters with Macramé inserts that are easily and quickly knotted are unusual. Select or dye cords that will coordinate with carpet, furniture, or bedspread tones. You may be able to repeat a fabric pattern in the knotting, and add beads that pick up colors in the scheme too. Paint the wood panels a contrasting or matching color. The panel (right) is painted in Illinois Bronze Daz-L colors that glow under black light, and four on a bedroom window are startling. (Dona Meilach)

8

Accessories for the Home

Macramé has proved versatile and extremely adaptable for home accessories. Knotted cords are striking when used for room dividers, panels, screens, chair covers, and even a decorative make-believe architectural column. Loosely knotted pieces may be worked over a lampshade and used as a light fixture.

A hammock, dining table accessories such as a tablecloth, placemats, and napkin rings may be knotted. The possibilities are unlimited once you put your imagination to work.

Macramé is beautiful for many types of window treatments; for valances, curtains, and patio door hangings which may be designed, like room dividers, so the knotting is worked from both sides and makes a visual statement whether seen from front or back. This type of hanging adapts beautifully to office entries where glass panels separate rooms; the Macramé is decorative from both sides; it also prevents people from the ever-present hazard of walking through a glass panel.

The ideas on the following pages may be copied. But more likely you will be stimulated to adapt them to Macramé projects for your own decorating needs.

Many household items can be renewed and enhanced by adding a knotted fringe or other parts to them. For example, a throw pillow with a knotted border can be coordinated to a curtain or drape with a knotted fringe, tieback, or valance.

Solid tapestry-like knotting can be incorporated with upholstery fabric and leather to re-cover a chair. Cut a rectangle, square, triangle, or other shape from the worn part of an upholstered piece of furniture, turn under a hem, and stitch a knotted panel into the worn area. On leather, you can punch holes in the material, then mount cords and work the knotting from the leather mounting. Use braided upholstery cord, available in many colors, jute, linen, or other cord that will wear well and match or contrast in color and texture.

Macramé chains are great for hanging large candles, plastic and ceramic plant pots from ceilings, trees, porches, or doorways. They're fun to live with and constant attention-getters. Also cover jars, bottles, wastebaskets, lamp bases, and bowls. Anything you want to take on a new look can be changed with the addition of attractively knotted cords.

Add further excitement to your decorative schemes by creating two- and three-dimensional Macramé forms for wall accessories and sculpture. See *Macramé: Creative Design in Knotting* by Dona Z. Meilach in the Crown Arts and Crafts Series.

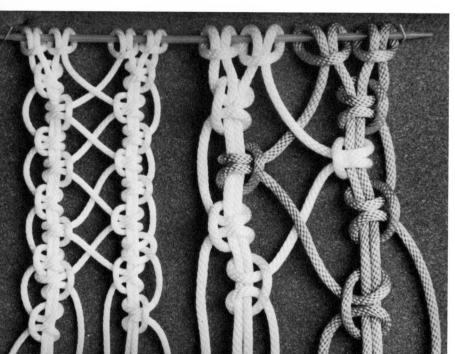

Let a Macramé bell hanging an-
nounce your visitors. This knotted
door ringer that is different, attrac-
tice, and practical has melodious
sheep bells added. It is knotted
with Lily Jute-tone in brown and
beige; it is in two sections each
from a short wood dowel, then the
top and bottom sections are joined.
The knot is the Alternating Lark's
Head Intertwine as demonstrated
below. (Susan Meilach)

The Alternating Lark's Head Intertwine is simply two sets of four cords
intertwined around each other's anchor cords. It is easier to follow in
the diagram than with a lengthy word description and is particularly
effective in two tones as in the doorbell above.

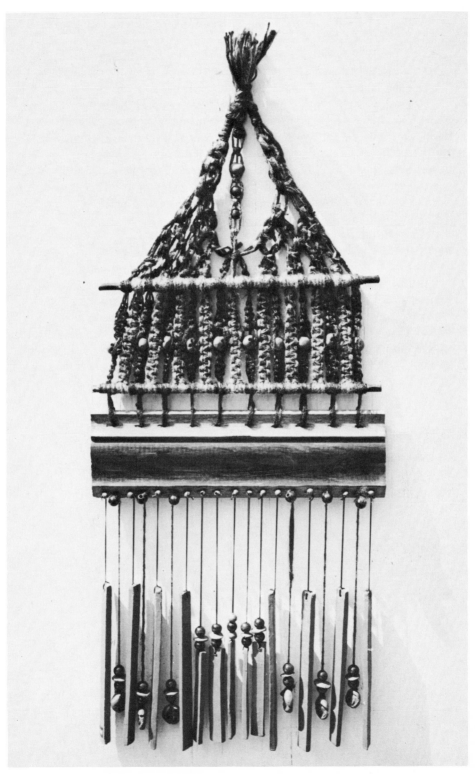

Wind chimes are another application for Macramé when combined with bamboo dowels and handmade ceramic beads. They tinkle gently when they are moved by the wind. (Eileen Knauf)

Macramé tablecloths and doilies are among historical evidence of this ancient craft; but most often, they were so closely and delicately knotted that it took expertise to differentiate knotting from lacemaking techniques. A Macramé tablecloth in the modern manner can be knotted in a relatively short time and be tremendously impressive for its utilitarian beauty. Ruth Hofferth knotted this cloth for use in a flower show, and the openwork area, using the Alterating Lark's Head Intertwine, is made to resemble the tulips she had displayed in an award-winning arrangement.

Overall diameter of the tablecloth from tip to tip of the knotted points of the overhang is 52 inches. She used 15 large balls of No. 24 white cotton seine twine and placed the finished cloth over a yellow satin circular liner.

The cloth is increased as you work by adding cords at each of the first three Clove Hitch Bars. It may be started on your knotting board, then the board taped to the table as you work. Or as the cloth size increases you can work over a shape of Celotex a fourth or a half the size of the table and move it as you work.

Original mounting consists of twelve sixteen-foot cords doubled to yield twenty-four 8-foot strands. These are Lark's Heads mounted on a large rubber washer for the center. See top detail (right) of beginning and knotting structure.

At the first Clove Hitch Bar from the center: add 24 ten-foot cords (48 strands) with Lark's Head and work in Square Knot sennits as shown. At top of tulip pattern add 55 eight-foot cords (110 strands) and tie all these cords into the tulip pattern (detail, bottom right) or your own design. At the bottom of the tulip pattern increase with 72 six-foot cords (144 strands) and continue in the Square Knot sennits, connecting them with the Alternating Square Knot about midway in the panel as shown.

Macramé tablecloth of white seine twine. (Ruth Hofferth)

Detail of central portion of tablecloth.

There is no increase at the rim, and the total number of knotting strands should be 254. Follow Alternating Square Knot pattern using 13 sets of four cords for each diamond shape. Allow four loose cords between each diamond panel. Gather the loose cords in each section with an Overhand Knot as shown.

Tablecloths may be knotted larger or smaller and in square or rectangular shapes. One knotter made a rectangular table runner which also doubled as a shoulder shawl. When knotting large projects, try to develop the pieces to knot from the center to each side so you will be working with half lengths of cords to make knotting easier.

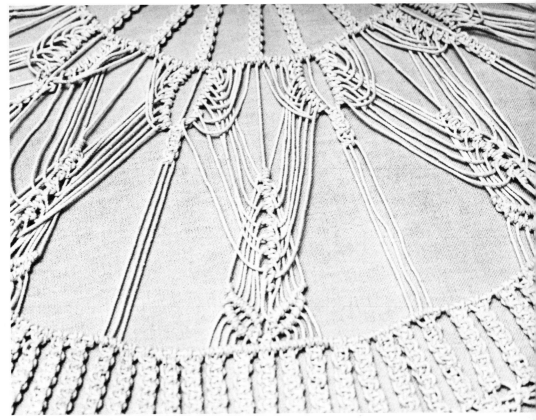

Detail of tulip design using Alternating Lark's Head Intertwine and a few sennits of Square Knots. At the bottom of each "tulip" Mrs. Hofferth worked in two leaf shapes by slightly curving the anchor cords of the Clove Hitch as she knotted.

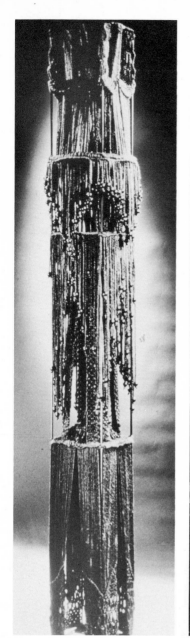 

Left. Perhaps this Macramé architectural column will add a new classification to the Ionic, Doric, and Corinthian orders. Working with square and round metal shapes, Ron Franks has created a new dimension for the avant-garde decorating scheme. Its height is floor to ceiling. It can be tied in monotone or multicolors using beads as an additional motif. All horizontal members are Clove Hitched. An interior column is structured with the Alternating Square Knot. Observe the large outer areas of floating cords. (Ron Franks)

Right. A hanging lampshade may be suspended over a light bulb, or a tube of plastic may be placed over the bulb to diffuse the light more evenly through the Macramé openings. The lampshade is actually knotted over two lampshade frames, one at the top and one at the bottom, then the knotting is continued. The Macramé is jute, readily available in any hardware store. The "beads" are fruit from a tree that have been dried and drilled. (Lois Spears)

Hanging planter for three pots is made from 32 natural jute cords doubled and mounted on a wood dowel. The Clove Hitched leaf pattern is tied by simply curving the anchor cords to resemble leaves. Strips are connected by carrying an anchor cord from one section into another and back again. Four short wood dowels are Clove Hitched to hold saucers of pots, and the knotting is continued around three-dimensionally. Cords are added on the bottom rods as needed. (Esther Parada)

Black Hammock of farmer's baler twine and an old hammock frame. Experience has shown that hammocks are best knotted from their long sides, rather than from the bar ends. This prevents the cords from stretching. (One hammock knotted at six feet stretched to double its length after only a few months' use.) The entire hammock is made of Alternating Square Knot sennits with short spacing cords added on outside edges and wrapped with nuts from a tree. (Detail left) (Lois Spears)

Headboard of differently knotted straps is mounted on a decorative rod. Straps hold pillows for backrest. Make the straps in the same way you would make a belt. Select cords that are not stretchy and tie knots close to prevent stretching. Straps pick up the colors in the bedspread. (Sally Davidson)

Room divider of heavy white seine twine is mounted on a brass rod with another rod at the bottom to hold it taut. Cords are draped and asymmetrically designed. Negative areas help provide the openness desired for a feeling of free space, yet a division of space. Shadows created by spatial hangings may be used effectively in decorating. Lighting on space dividers should be considered. 80 inches long, 40 inches wide. (Estelle Carlson)

Guitar strap of jute should be knotted quite tightly to prevent stretching. The area that is to fit over the shoulder should be of flatter knots so they don't dig in. Twists and raised areas may be knotted front and back. Begin with 12 strands from a gathered Overhand Knot and attach to the guitar without interfering with the guitar strings. (Lois Spears)

Hanging plastic wildflower pot with six Macramé straps of Clove Hitch Chains and Square Knots, and Overhand Knots. Begin with cords mounted over a plastic ring at the bottom. Depending upon the size of the pot, make cords the necessary length for graceful hanging, then gather all cords at the top and knot. Add a bead and hanging clip. The same idea can be used for ceramic and glass jars and large candles. Hanging straps can also be made separately, knotted beneath the pot, and the ends strung with beads. (Dona Meilach)

Napkin rings are fun and fast to knot. Make several strips as one knotting panel, then cut the strips apart. Mount 22 cords, doubled, with Clove Hitches onto a holding line of another cord or a knitting needle. Allow about an inch of floating cords and make a first row of Clove Hitches over a new 16-inch anchor cord. Tie two or three Half Knots with each group of four strands from one side of the work to the other. Then mount another 16-inch anchor cord and tie another row of Clove Hitches. This completes the first band of the first napkin ring. Allow about one inch of floating cords and begin the same pattern of one Clove Hitch Bar, two or three Half Knots, and another Clove Hitch Bar until you reach the end of the cords. Cut the rings apart carefully halfway between the floating cords that separate each band. Fluff all ends.

To tie the ring together, turn to the wrong side and tie Square Knots tightly with the two anchor cord endings on each side. Cut off excess length, turn the ring right-side out, and fluff. It is not finished. For the original mounted ring, remove the holding cord, undo the Lark's Head, cut at the loop, and fluff out. (Stewart Purinton)

Place mats may be made of rough or finely textured cords for informal or formal dining. They are practical because they are almost indestructible. You can wash them and pull to shape. Shown is a mat of natural manilla cord worked in Alternating Square Knots and chevron design Clove Hitches, with fringed ends. Mat measures 18 inches long, 8½ inches wide and is worked with a 1/2-pound ball or 110 yards of 1/8-inch-diameter cord cut into 7-foot lengths. Begin by pinning the ends of the cord to the knotting board, allowing a 3-inch length for unraveling, then Clove Hitching over a separate anchor cord for the beginning row. The loose ends of the anchor cord are bent up and become part of the fringing. Follow pattern connecting the Clove Hitch strips with the anchor cord. Add another anchor cord for the bottom Clove Hitch Bar. For a table runner, simply make the piece longer. (Collection: Dona Meilach)

Bottles covered with Macramé are beautiful and fun to work. Begin with cords at the top and increase as necessary. To finish at bottom, bring cords under and knot around a circle with a Clove Hitch. Cut ends close, tuck under, and glue. A circle of felt will camouflage the endings and provide a finished appearance. (Spike Africa)

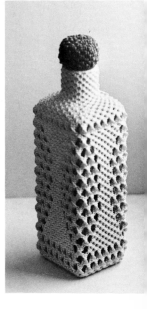

9 More Knots and Knotting Hints

Along with the Clove Hitch and Square Knot, it is helpful to know the auxiliary knots often used in Macramé, wrapping methods, and how to add cords when they shorten.

WRAPPING A COIL

a. *Finished wrapped coil using one of four cords to wrap. Any multiples may be used.*
b. *With the end of one cord, begin wrapping at bottom of the coil. Overlap the first wrap to prevent the coil from slipping, and continue winding.*
c. *Wrap large-eye needle into the coil with the eye at the top. At the end of the number of wraps desired, thread the loose end through the needle.*
d. *Pull the needle through all the wraps to the bottom. Tighten the coil by twisting gently. Cut the ends to even lengths if desired.*

Cords may be wrapped from top to bottom and the loose end pulled from bottom to top of the cord, then cut and glued.

For cords that are too thick to thread through a needle, wrap loosely and push the end back down through the wraps. Tighten.

Another way to wrap is to mount a doubled cord with a Lark's Head to the group of strands to be wrapped. Continue to wrap both strands of the added cord around the group. Slip the ends of the cord up through the last two wraps, snip close. Glue to hold.

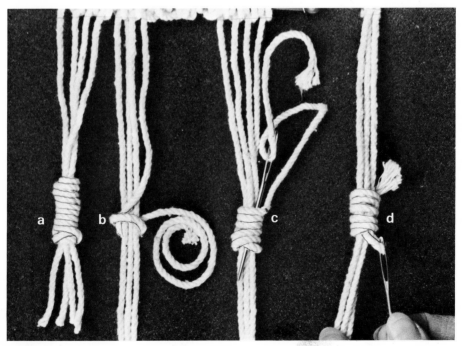

Wrapping is a technique for attractively finishing loose cord ends so they do not dangle wildly or pull out.

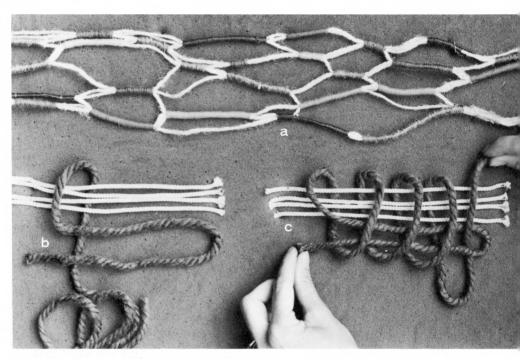

Another wrapping method is referred to as Peruvian Wrapping. Use it when you do not have a needle. Use it for wrapping a new cord color over a group of cords, and for thick cords that will not fit through a needle eye.

a.   *Example of different color cords wrapped around jute lengths within a belt design.*

b.   *Lay out the strands to be wrapped: Place the left end of the cord in U shape parallel to strands: bring the right end over, around, and under the strands and under the U shape as shown.*

c.   *Continue to wind tightly until you are near bottom of the U. (A loose wind is shown for demonstration purposes but the winds should be tight and close together.) On the last wind, bring the right end through the U and hold with a finger. Pull the left end up, release your finger, and the right end will travel up with the pull to tighten the wrap. Cut the ends close to wrap and tuck under if necessary. (Belt detail and method: Ursula MacPherson)*

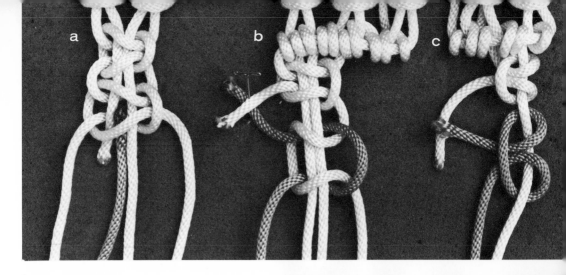

ADDING CORDS

When cords shorten while knotting, they may be added unobtrusively in several ways. Fabric glues will aid in splicing and holding the ends at the underside of the work.

a. *If one cord shortens in a Square Knot, add a new cord between the anchors. Drop the short cord and continue knotting with the longer cord.*

b. *New cord is added at the edge or within the work as a knotting cord. Loose ends may later be woven into the back of the work, knotted, and stitched or spliced by gluing.*

c. *New cord added on a vertical strand with a Lark's Head.*

d. *Add a cord that may have been underestimated or introduce a new cord by adding it to a Clove Hitch Bar. Simply overlap the anchors and continue to Clove Hitch.*

e. *Adding an anchor cord for a new Clove Hitch Bar will help keep all the knotting cords even. (When a side cord is picked up to be used as an anchor it will shorten quickly.) New anchor cords may be extended and additional cords Clove Hitched to expand a shape.*

f. *Another way to increase within a pattern of Alternate Square Knots provides an interesting surface detail. Simply make an Overhand Knot at the doubled portion of the new cord, insert it between the Square Knots as shown and the tension of the Square Knot will hold the new cord in place. This can be used only with closely tied Square Knots.*

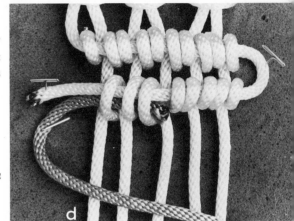

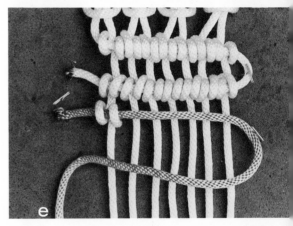

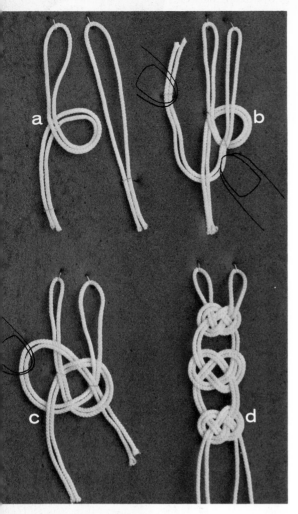

JOSEPHINE KNOT

Patterns with Josephine Knots are found throughout the book: Josephine Knots may be used for entire pieces, for portions within a pattern, and as a relief from Square Knots and Clove Hitches. Josephine Knots have been used in belts, ties, ponchos, vests, and skirt patterns. They may be tied loosely or tightly. Two cords (four strands) are used for the demonstration, but you can use any number of cords.

a. *Make a loop, as shown, with the left cords.*
b. *Bring the right cords over the left loop and under the loose left strands.*
c. *Bring the right cords around and over the top left, under the next pair of cords, over the right cords and under the original loop in the same way you would weave: over, under, over and under.*
d. *Pull to even and begin a loop for the next knot. If the cords tend to turn, begin every other knot with the right cord by simply reversing the procedure. A dab of glue behind the cords will keep the knots set.*

OVERHAND KNOT

The Overhand Knot is a versatile knot used within a pattern, at ends, to hold beads in place, and as a design with other cords. Simply make a loop and bring one end around the cord through the loop and pull. It may be intertwined using one cord for each knot. It may also be tied with four cords or more.

SQUARE KNOT BUTTON

Button Knots are important for many accessories that require buttonhole closings including neckwear, clothes, purses, and belts. The Square Knot Button, sometimes called the "Popcorn Knot" may be used for closings, but because it has an open center, it can be used for lacing and for a raised surface detail.

a. *Finished Square Knot Button.*
b. *Tie a minimum of three Square Knots (more for higher buttons). Bring the two anchor cords up over the knots and between the anchor cords at the top. Pull through to form the raised area. Continue as at bottom of (a).*

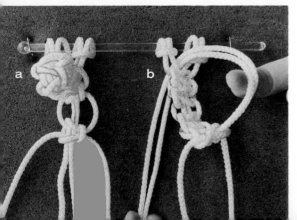

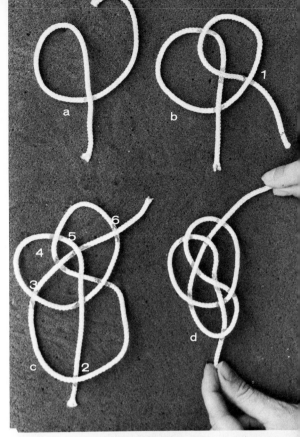

ENGLISH BUTTON

The English Button may be used as a flat decorative motif or, when pulled tightly, it will bunch up into a knot that may be used as button or as an ending.

a. *Loop the cord as shown, allowing more length on the right end.*
b. *Make another loop in the right cord overlapping the first loop and place the end under cord at 1.*
c. *Bring the right cord over left end at 2, under first loop at 3, then weave over at 4, under at 5, and over at 6.*
d. *Carefully pull cords, one end at a time, to tighten. Do not try to pull both ends simultaneously, or the knot will bunch up. Cords must be worked into place.*

The English Button's appearance can differ depending upon how it is tied and whether it is used within a design as a flat motif, or at an end as a three-dimensional button. It can also be made in a separate cord, then stitched or knotted into the work for raised button closings. Knots alone may be used for cuff links, earrings, and pins. (Thanks to Ursula MacPherson)

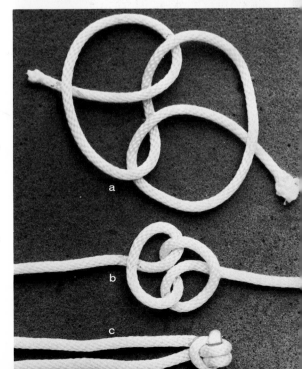

TURK'S HEAD KNOT

The Turk's Head Knot may be used in the center of a cord, as a button, or as an ending knot.

a. *Place the cords as shown.*
b. *Pull each end and leave flat for a suspended knot.*
c. *Pull tightly for a button or ending knot. A knot can also be made in an independent cord, then knotted in or stitched to work for a button. (Thanks to Joan Michaels Paque)*

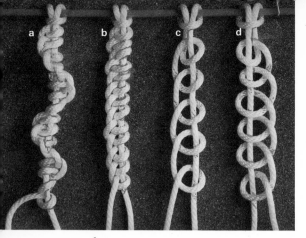

1

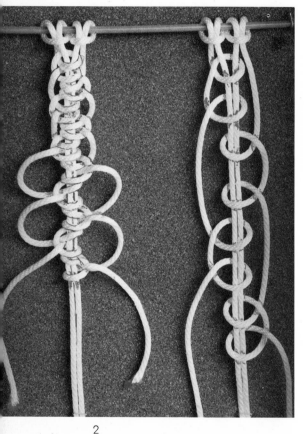

2

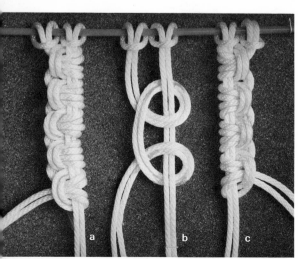

3

CHAINS

Chains are interesting motifs to tie into belts, jewelry, and other accessories. Usually the knotting cords shorten more rapidly than the anchor cords, so mount the cords unevenly when you know you will be working with chains.

CLOVE HITCH TWISTING CHAIN (1)

One of the easiest variations of the Clove Hitch is the chain. Using two strands, continue tying the Clove Hitch on one side only of the other strand. Begin with the first loop over the anchor cord and continue tying the loops over the anchor strand as shown. (a) The cord will twist or (b) it may be worked to lie flat and curve. (c) Tie with the left strand over the right for the entire length or (d) the right strand over the left. The knotting strand will be used up more rapidly than the anchor, so figure and mount lengths unevenly when making these chains. For bulky effects knot the Clove Hitches over several anchor cords.

ALTERNATING CLOVE HITCH CHAIN (2)

For this chain, tie both loops of the Clove Hitch over the anchor cord, first with the left strand, then with the right strand. For a variation, accentuate the curve that results between the knots for another design motif. Try putting beads on these curves for another surface treatment.

SINGLE VERTICAL
LARK'S HEAD CHAIN (3)

The Lark's Head chain may be tied with two cords or four as illustrated. It doesn't matter which cords are used for knotting, the right or left.

a. *Illustrates knotting the left cords over the anchor to result in a ridge on the left side. (c) has a right side ridge resulting from knotting the right cords over the anchor cords.*

b. *To make the Vertical Lark's Head, bring the cord over the anchor, make the loop around to the top, and bring the cord through. For the second loop, begin with the cord under the anchor, loop it around over the anchor and through the curve. Correctly tied, the knot will have a ridge over the two loops.*

PICOTS

Picots are small loops that extend above the holding line as a decorative edging for purses, neckwear, vests, and other accessories.

SINGLE LOOP PICOT (1)

The simplest way to begin a Picot is shown finished (left) and the procedure (right). Mount each cord to be used onto a holding line. Tie the first strand with a Clove Hitch, then pin a loop at the desired height above the holding line to the knotting board and tie the second strand with a Clove Hitch. The result will be a series of loops above the holding line. This is the principle of Picots, regardless of how complex the knots are in the loop above the line. Evolve your own knots for Picot decorations.

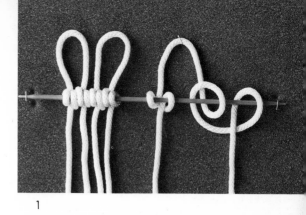

1

MULTIPLE LOOP PICOT (2)

A series of loops in varying sizes makes an attractive border. Use one or more cords. Pin the three loops to the board as shown. Place a holding line over the strands and Clove Hitch them.

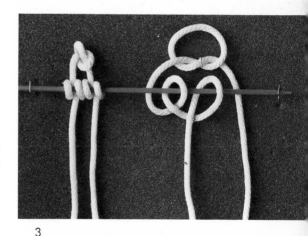

2

OVERHAND KNOT PICOT (3)

A more decorative Picot can be made by tying an Overhand Knot in the loop before Clove Hitching the second strand.

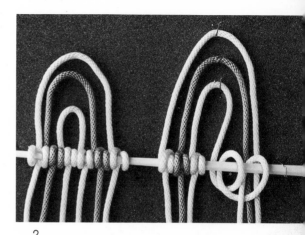

3

WEAVING MOTIFS (4)

Weaving cords within a section of knotting adds another attractive area to a surface. Here cords are woven within a Clove Hitch diamond. Use a crochet hook to pull the cords over and under one another in the weaving progression.

Supply Sources

The following supply sources are listed for your convenience. They have been selected because they answered correspondence within five days to three weeks. They carry a varied selection of merchandise. No endorsement or responsibility by the author is implied. Letter references used are:

B. Beads and other jewelry items
C. Cords, yarns, a wide selection
D. Dyes
F. Feathers
H. Hardware: buckles, purse handles, fastenings
Cg. Charge for catalog or sample cards which may be submitted with inquiry or after mailing is received.

C	Ace Hardware local outlets	B,F	Grey Owl Indian Craft Co. 150–02 Beaver Road Jamaica, Queens, N.Y. 11433
C	Briggs & Little Woolen Mills York Mills, Harvey Station, N.B., Canada	C,H	P. C. Herwig 264 Clinton Street Brooklyn, N.Y. 11201
C,D Cg. .50	Countryside Handweavers West Elkhorn Ave. Box 1743 Estes Park, Col. 80517	C	House of Yarns and Fabrics Box 98 Hampton, N.H. 03842
C Cg. .50	Creative Handweavers P. O. Box 26480 Los Angeles, Calif. 90026	B,C,H Cg. .50	International Handcraft & Supply 103 Lyndon Street Hermosa Beach, Calif. 90254
B Cg. .50	Earthy Endeavors 13441 Camellia St. Whittier, Calif. 90602	B,H	Jewelart, Inc. 7753 Densmore Ave. Van Nuys, Calif. 91406 (and local outlets)
B Stoneware	Earthworks 624 W. Willow Street Chicago, Ill. 60614	B,C,H	The Knit & Knot Shop 2701 North 21st Street Tacoma, Wash. 98406
C	Esther Fear's 1807 Central Street Evanston, Ill. 60201	C	Lily Mills Co. Department HWH Shelby, N.C. 28150
C	Frederick J. Fawcett 129 South Street Boston, Mass. 02111		
B,H	Gloria's Glass Garden Box 1990 Beverly Hills, Calif. 90213	B,C,H Cg. .50	Macramé & Weaving Supply 63 East Adams Street Chicago, Ill. 60603
Hand spinning wool	Greentree Ranch Wools Route 3, Box 461 Loveland, Col. 80537	B,C Cg. .25	Jeane Malsada Box 28182 Atlanta, Ga. 30328

B,C Cg. .50	The Mannings R.D. 2 East Berlin, Pa. 17316	B,C	Walco Products, Inc. 1200 Zerega Avenue Bronx, N.Y. 10462
C,D Cg. .50	Northwest Handcraft House 110 West Esplanade N. Vancouver, B. C. Canada	B,C,D,F,H	Warp, Woof & Potpourri 514 North Lake Ave. Pasadena, Calif. 91101
C	Pacific Fibre & Rope Co., Inc. 903 Flint Ave. Wilmington, Calif. 90744	B,C	The Weaver's Loft 320 Blue Bell Road Williamstown, N. J. 08094
B Stoneware	Sondra Savage 425 Narcissus Corona del Mar, Calif. 92625	B,C	Weaving Workshop 3324 N. Halsted Street Chicago, Ill. 60608
B,C,H	Tandy Leather Co. (local outlets)	C	Wellington Puritan Mills, Inc. P. O. Box 22185 Louisville, Ky. 40222 (local
B,C	Threads, Rip Neal 9621 Seeley Lake Drive Tacoma, Wash. 98499		outlets; school order over $50 through the Mills)
B	Three Gables Homecrafts 1825 Charleston Beach Bremerton, Wash. 98310	C,D	The Yarn Depot 545 Sutter Street San Francisco, Calif. 94102
B,C	Walbead 38 W. 37th Street New York, N. Y. 10018	B,C,H	The Yarn Merchant 8533 Beverly Blvd. Los Angeles, Calif. 90048

Index